M000303753

A PRISONER OF JESUS CHRIST

JIMMY E. WINDHAM

8-3-21

To: Karen

From: Jimmy Windham

May God always bless you!

Copyright © 2019
Jimmy E. Windham
All rights reserved

No part of this book may be reproduced or transmitted or transferred in any form or by any means, graphic, electronic, mechanical, including photocopying, recording, taping, or by any information storage retrieval system or device, without the permission in writing by the author.

The author has tried to recreate events, locales and conversations from his memories of them. In order to maintain their anonymity, in some instances he has changed the names of individuals and places, and some identifying characteristics and details such as physical properties, occupations and places of residence.

Although the author and publisher have made every effort to ensure that the information in this book was correct at press time, the author and publisher do not assume and hereby disclaim any liability to any party for any loss, damage, or disruption caused by errors or omissions, whether such errors or omissions result from negligence, accident, or any other cause.

Cover Concept: Jimmy E Windham
Cover Design: Rev. Al King
Cover Photography: Gina Marie Fountain
Cover Typography: Sharon Kizziah-Holmes

Publishing Coordinator – Sharon Kizziah-Holmes

Paperback-Press
an imprint of A & S Publishing
A & S Holmes, Inc.

ISBN -13: 978-1-945669-81-1

CONTENTS

Acknowledgments i

Chapter 1 1

Chapter 2 13

Chapter 3 19

Chapter 4 25

Chapter 5 29

Chapter 6 35

Chapter 7 41

Chapter 8 47

Chapter 9 57

Chapter 10 63

Chapter 11 71

Chapter 12 77

Chapter 13 85

Chapter 14 97

Chapter 15 105

Chapter 16 113

Chapter 17 123

Chapter 18 131

Chapter 19 139

Chapter 20 145

Chapter 21 157

Chapter 22 165

Chapter 23 169

Chapter 24 181

Chapter 25 187

Chapter 26 195

Chapter 27 201

Chapter 28 205

Chapter 29 209

Chapter 30 223

ACKNOWLEDGMENTS

I would like to personally thank the following people, for without their love, care, prayers and friendship, this book wouldn't have been possible. So, thank you all and God bless you:

Dr. Thad and Jeannette Davis in Florence, South Carolina; Mr. Sonny and Marilyn Veit in Standish, Michigan; Mr. David Harmon in Newberry, South Carolina; Brother Alfred and Colleen King in McMinnville, Tennessee; People of the Living God Church in Tennessee; Brother Del and Sister Audrey Hubbard in Ferndale, Washington; Ms. Becky Britton Volz in Springfield, Missouri, for her tireless effort in making this project go forward; Ms. Noella Thomas in Missouri for all her dedication and work to make this book project possible. Thank you all for all your support in my life. God bless you.

Also, I want to thank my five children for your forgiveness and love: Jennifer Sipper, Shelley Brown, Jimmy Windham, Jr., Billy Windham, and David Windham. Also, thank you Mama (Mrs. Leila Stroud), and thank you Carolyn Davis, my sister in Utah. God bless you all.

CHAPTER 1

I looked up and a policeman was standing in front of my car with his .38 pointed at me. Then I looked to my open door and another .38 was pointed at me. I was sitting behind the steering wheel in a deep haze like nothing was real.

He said, "Ease your hands to your steering wheel, because if you move them anywhere but there, I'll blow your brains out. Do you understand me?"

I thought I was dreaming. Then I felt a handcuff hit my left arm, click closed, then he pulled me out of my car, and turned me around beside my car as the other policeman held his gun on me and finished handcuffing me behind my back. I don't remember anything more until the next day when I woke up in a jail cell.

I walked to the bars to look around. I had no idea why I was in jail but across from my cell was a man in a cell looking at me. I asked him, "What am I doing here?"

He said, "Man, they got you on a murder charge!"

I said, "You're crazy, who'd I kill?"

He said, "They say you killed a man over a woman."

* * *

I was raised in a very dysfunctional home with a dad who would go to church for a year, and during that time he'd take me to small towns where he'd stand on a street corner with his Bible, and begin to preach. The next year he'd spend drinking, running around with women and beating my mom. I had two older brothers and one younger sister.

Being poor, I had to sleep with my two older brothers. Our shotgun house had only one coal heater and it was in the living room; so, many nights I woke up with no covers because my two bigger brothers pulled it onto themselves.

Dad would leave us and be gone for months at a time. Once when I was five, he was going through one of his tantrums, and he and Mom were fussing about his drinking. I watched as he began cutting his throat with a double-edged razor. When I saw blood running down his shirt, I yelled at him to please stop. I was too young to know that he hadn't really injured himself, but was just making my mom pity him.

When I was six and school was out for the season, Daddy came out of the house with a suitcase, leaving my mom sitting on the porch. As he walked away, I ran behind him and he took my hand. We thumbed rides from town to town until we came to a small town named Ridgeland, South Carolina, and he went to a church and talked to the pastor. The pastor put us up in a spare bedroom. I believe now that Daddy only took me with him because someone with a small child could get help easier. Daddy told the pastor that he was a preacher, so the pastor asked him to preach that night.

Now, some may not believe that a six-year-old boy can remember details I'm about to tell you, but I remember clearly the first time my heart was touched by God's Son. That old pastor preached hellfire-and-brimstone, spitting while he preached.

He scared me at first and I snuggled closer to my daddy, but then the strangest thing happened. As he preached, he teared up saying that everyone needs a Savior. I listened

2

intently as he told how this Man died in our place so we wouldn't have to burn in the fire he preached about. He said that Man was God's Son and wanted to come into our hearts. He pointed to me and said "even this child needs a savior to save him from hell."

I didn't know where it was, but I knew I didn't want to go there.

Then he said, "If you want to go to Heaven you need to run to this altar and let Jesus come into your heart."

As I watched people going down to the front and bowing at two benches, he said this Jesus loved me, so I slipped out of my seat and went and bowed down before the altar. I felt a strong desire to ask this Jesus to save me, and I wept as I told Him that this preacher said I needed a savior.

After everyone sat back down, I could still hear that old preacher's words, "That little boy was touched by God's Spirit tonight because you can still see his tears on the altar." That was my first experience with the Lord.

At home, the terror and emptiness I felt got worse because my brother Clifton began to act a lot like my dad. When Daddy was upset for any reason, he'd grab me, pull off his thick belt and beat me all across my back, my head, and my legs until big blood welts appeared.

Around the age of eleven, Clifton began showing signs of homosexuality. I had to sleep in the same bed with him, and many nights I had to fight him off and run in the cold to the couch where there were no covers but my coat. But he and my kid sister, Carolyn, were my mom's "pets," and he could do no wrong in her eyes.

If I tried to tell her how Cliff was abusing me and Carolyn, then the next day while Mom and Daddy were at work, Clifton would terrorize my sister and me. He became violent at a moment's notice, so I was always afraid to be around him. Even if Mom and Dad were home, and he didn't get his way, like winning at Old Maid, he'd give me that leering look which I knew meant, "I'll get you tomorrow when Mom's not here to protect you."

Each morning I'd try to get up before him, and I'd go crawl under the house which was held up by brick columns, and I'd hide all day without eating anything. I had a little dog named Blackie who seemed to know how I felt because, as I laid there on the cold ground crying, he'd lay beside me and lick my face.

I now know that I was in a state of severe depression; and because I couldn't eat anything, my mom fed me sugared biscuits and sweet tea. My growth was stunted because of this, and it made me the smallest kid in my class. I really loved my little sister and because of her being the youngest and the only girl, she was always with Mom. That made Clifton jealous of Carolyn and he started terrorizing her too.

There was one beautiful summer morning, when Clifton, who was so devious and sly he'd cause me to let my guard down, acted friendly and he wanted us to play house, so he dressed up in Mom's clothes. Because he was "Mama," he made us clean the house and wash the dishes, which were his chores. Mine was cutting the grass or all the outside chores. Carolyn and I did this.

Then he said once we were finished, he'd take us fishing. He knew that I loved the outdoors, and when we went fishing, I could pull a Red Breast Brim out of a mud hole in the front yard so to speak. We would walk down to a small stream called Smith Swamp. Clifton's face changed instantly from Dr. Jekyll to Mr. Hyde. Carolyn and I were in front of him down the bank next to the fast running stream so we had no chance to run away like we usually did. He grabbed Carolyn and said, "Jimmy, grab her other arm or you'll be next." Not knowing what he meant and being so scared of him, I obeyed.

Bear in mind that he was two years older than me and he outweighed me by many pounds (he ate the best out of all of us kids), and I wasn't much taller than my sister who was four years younger. I stood holding the only person in the world I really loved by her little arm.

Clifton grabbed her leg and told me to grab her other leg, so I did. He began swinging her back and forth towards the fast-moving stream and said on three let her go. I heard him tell her, "Remember when Mama brought you that chocolate milk yesterday and you wouldn't let me have any? Well, I planned this all night and now you'll pay." Still swinging her, I heard "one, two, three" and I let go.

I can't even begin to know how that seven-year-old girl felt, but I know this: it traumatized her for life, only her love for God then and now pulled her through. She's never let me forget that it was I who let go. I know now it was wrong, but, honestly, being a little kid, I didn't know what to do. I believe if I hadn't, the situation would've been worse.

He changed instantly and began babying her and told her, "I told you he didn't love you, and I do. So now, give me some chocolate milk when you get it." With his arm around her, they started up the bank as I just stood there trying to figure out what just happened. When they were crossing the bridge, he looked down at me and said, "Now, she's mine. Leave her alone." That didn't last long, because soon he was back to his devilish ways and abusing her during the day.

In Marion, where we were raised, they built a recreation center and kids could frequent it all day, so I asked Mom if I could take Carolyn the next day.

She said, "Yes."

One of the worst feelings of my life that I can remember so vividly is that next morning I tiptoed into Mom's bedroom where she and Carolyn slept in a twin bed. My dad slept in a full-sized bed alone. I gently awakened my sister and whispered, "Hurry up and get dressed. We're going to play all day." (Which gave us such joy!)

She did, so we snuck out of the house. About a block down the street I looked back and Clifton was running after us. Terror hit me as I'm sure it did her. I grabbed her arm and almost dragged her as we ran, but soon he caught us and grabbed her.

I saw pure terror on her face as she kept screaming, "Jimmy, Jimmy, help me."

I stayed back from them so he couldn't grab me, and I cursed at him, threw rocks at him, and begged him to let her go. Even back at the house, I stayed outside all day begging him to let her go. I remember telling him, "Clifton, one day when I get big, I'm going to kill you."

He'd laugh his smirky laugh and said, "You'll be nothing

but a runt little boy."

My Dad had us going to the Pentecostal Holiness Church across the street, a four-walled wooden building with a dirt floor covered in sawdust and with wooden benches with no backs. He had "gotten religion" again. But it didn't seem to help Clifton.

Another day as Clifton and I were walking home from school we came upon a house with a kitten on the porch. Next to the house was a big open field, with a large thicket of woods in the middle.

Clifton stole the kitten and I began to pet it. He told me to follow him as he walked toward the thicket. Once there he began to throw the kitten up into the air. I still had no idea what he was up to, and maybe he didn't plan it, but it seemed that evil just came on him instantly.

The kitten, now afraid for its life, scratched him as it tried to cling to him, so he threw it against a tree. The kitten instantly stopped moving and blood came out its eyes and nose. Clifton picked up a stick about two inches around and a foot long and he beat that kitten until it was flat. I was screaming at him to stop, but it only made him laugh. Then he grabbed me and said, "Here take this stick and beat that cat so you won't tell on me, or I'll beat you with it." I remember crying as I beat that kitten a few times and then we walked home.

My older brother Hal was two years older than Clifton, but not as heavy, so Clifton would almost get the best of him. I think Clifton was a little afraid to push Hal too much though because Hal finally had enough of Clifton's meanness. Clifton who was a librarian at school was more of a big sissy.

I only have good memories of Hal. Hal played high school baseball and when I became a teenager and started playing baseball, Hal saw my abilities as a left-handed pitcher. By this time, we lived in the country, so he began to teach me to pitch, throwing the ball back and forth in the back yard. Hal had a catcher's mitt, and he'd squat and let me throw as hard as I could as he caught the ball.

Even though most boys my age were much taller and bigger than me, I had a natural ability to throw a baseball hard and straight. I was wiry and strong because a few years earlier, to get away from Clifton during the day, I'd walk a couple of miles down our dirt road that led into the main road to Florence. And across the main road my uncle owned a country store where you could buy gas, groceries, drinks, and beer. At that time, I was 11 years old.

I'd go pump gas for my Uncle Gene all day. He'd give me a big thick slice of bologna with a lot of mayonnaise on two slices of fresh white bread to eat for my lunch and a pint of chocolate milk, and he'd pay me with a big heavy fifty cent piece. For a small boy, I felt rich. I always bought chips, sodas, and candy with it and took it home to my siblings, especially for Clifton because it made him leave me alone. At times, I still had to sneak away or run from him, but by now he couldn't catch me. I was short and little, but fast.

I remember this one particular morning he caught me in the bedroom and he pushed me in a corner and would slap me and beat on me as I tried to run. I was no match for him so finally I slumped down in the corner and cried. He'd laugh, "Jimmy's a cry baby," over and over. That weekend my dad took me to his brother Gene's store to work. My dad was drinking again and he, Uncle Gene, and the farmers all around there would drink, laugh, and lie.

(My Uncle Gene had been a boxer in the Golden Gloves when he was young and had fought in the Army Air Corps where he also was a fighter pilot in World War II. I looked up to him because his stories were about his bravery as a pilot who shot down German planes when he was stationed in Britain. I'd hang my arms over the counter and just stare intently when he had the floor. Behind his store he had put up a boxing ring, and at times he would go out and spar with his friends. He never lost and I wanted to be just like him.)

At any rate, that day he saw I had a black eye and asked me how I got it. I remember lying because I couldn't tell on Clifton or I'd really get a beating later. I made up a story about three big boys at school and of course I beat them all; but in the process, I got the black eye.

He told me, "Son, I'm gonna teach you to fight," and for the next few months as my daddy ran the store, he had me

7

outside punching a heavy bag and sparring with him. He would have me come almost every day and he trained me on footwork, counter punching, jabbing with my right and following through with all my weight with my left until finally I could master the speed bag which taught me to have good reflexes.

One day he asked, "Jimmy, where did you really get that black eye?"

I broke down and told him how Clifton had treated me and my sister since I was eight or nine. He said, "Son, one day you'll be able to beat him, but until then keep punching that bag."

By now my self-esteem and confidence were growing because my Uncle Gene was pumping me full of himself. He was a braggart and between him and my dad I learned revenge and violence.

At times, some of the black sharecroppers would come to get gas, a few groceries and play checkers at the side of Uncle Gene's store as they drank beer. As I pumped gas my dad and Uncle Gene would say, "I bet you $5 you can put your boy in that ring outside and my nephew who's smaller will run him out of the ring."

They'd bring their son that next day and he and I would pull our shirts and shoes off. I never remember fighting any boy that I didn't have to look up to, so the first time they did this, I told my uncle I didn't want to fight, but he said, "So you want to be a sissy like Clifton, and let him run over you all your life? Go home, boy, and don't come back." His words hurt and by now I could cuss real good so I uttered a few cuss words about calling me a sissy.

He tied those gloves on me and put me in that ring, and that boy and I began to slug it out. My uncle was shouting commands at me while this young boy who had no training was on the receiving end of all the violence, I could throw at him. After a few rounds, he didn't want to fight me anymore.

One day while fighting a kid, my uncle introduced me to a friend of his, Mr. Marion Galloway, who was the manager of the Florence Recreation Center. He had bragged on me, so Mr. Galloway had come to watch me fight that day.

Mr. Galloway was one of the promoters for the Pee Dee Area Golden Gloves Association, so I really wanted to impress him. When this kid and I were put in the ring and the bell rang I showed off all the skills and tactics I'd learned and easily won. When I was fighting in the ring, I had no fear of anyone. But I was terrified of Clifton's laugh and voice.

One day Hal and I were outside throwing the baseball back and forth. Clifton came outside and stopped us because he said he had a present to give to Hal or me. I believe Hal did it to protect me so he said, "Okay, give it to me."

Clifton said, "Okay, hold your hand out and close your eyes." When Hal held out his hand I watched in horror as Clifton took a single edged razor blade and split Hal's hand open. I ran away as fast as I could. Hal had to go to the hospital and have stitches put in his hand.

For the first time, I saw my Daddy grab Clifton when he got back home and beat him with a belt without Mama trying to stop him or step in. That was the last time I can remember Hal and me playing ball together because he was afraid Clifton would get jealous.

I did go on to play Little League that year and the next, and each year I was picked for the all-star team because of my abilities to pitch fast and straight. Later on, I played Pony League then Colt League ball.

Soon after the fight that Mr. Galloway watched, he and my Uncle Gene drove me over to Florence to fight in the Golden Glove division. It was a fight I'll never forget, because it changed me. In Florence, they have a home for troubled boys. It was those boys we local boys had to fight and they were well-fed and well-trained.

I was used to fighting local boys who had no training so I won every fight. I watched all those boys fight before it was my turn and they didn't lose. They had been running for miles before breakfast and afterwards they worked out in their gym for hours. I found this out a year later when I was sent there myself.

I'll get to that; but now they called my name to go fight a boy named Dexter Coker from, if I remember correctly,

Hartsville, South Carolina. He was taller than me. We started fighting in the first of three three-minute rounds, and I held my ground as I tried remembering what my Uncle Gene said to do. At the same time my Uncle and Marion Galloway who were both in my corner were screaming instructions at me until I didn't know what to do, so I just fought to keep him off me. He won by a decision. But the next day's paper called it the fight of the night. It said, "Left handed Jimmy Windham looked down the gloves of Dexter for three rounds but punched and counter punched until Dexter's attacks became fewer and further between as both boys fought to win."

Afterwards when my uncle drove us back to Marion, he told me how proud he was of me. I remember telling him, "But I lost that fight and I'll never lose again." To this day I've never lost another fight in the ring or a fist fight in a bar. I had gotten so good with my fists that twice in my life I fought three men at one time who tried to harm me.

The reason for going to the South Carolina Industrial School for Boys in Florence the next year was because of this: My home life was a mess. Dad no longer took us to church and was back to drinking, fussing, running around on my mom, and occasionally beating her. In all my life, I've never seen my mom smoke a cigarette or drink a beer. She would try hard to be a good mother. I remember one year, for the first time, she called the Salvation Army to tell them she couldn't afford to give us a Christmas, so they brought us kids toys and food because Dad was gone again.

When he came back that year, I couldn't find any peace. Something was gnawing at me inside my heart and I wanted to die. I was 13 years old, I had failed the sixth grade and had to take it over, and that year I failed the seventh grade and was told I had to take it over the next year. I was so depressed for a 13-year-old kid that one day when I was walking home from school I stopped on a corner at the main fast-moving street and I walked out in front of a car. The driver saw me so he swerved left to miss me but the front fender of his car hit my left arm and leg and spun me around and I went down in the street but wasn't seriously hurt. He stopped, he and a woman passenger ran back to me to see how badly I was hurt. They picked me up and tried to take me to the hospital to be checked but I refused to go. When they knew I was truly okay, just shook up, they left. Still I couldn't shake that feeling of wanting to die. Many times, I asked God to let me die so I could go to Heaven, but He didn't hear me. I thought I had to go on living in what I called hell. I felt like my soul was being pulled in so many directions until I would go in my bedroom and look up and scream. I remember feeling like nobody loved me, God wouldn't let me die, and He didn't love me or want me in Heaven with Him.

CHAPTER 2

On my 14th birthday Mama gave me my first birthday party. I invited my schoolmates, and the only one who showed was my best friend (probably only friend) Charles S. who still lives in Marion.

Mama had given me a dollar for my birthday, so that night I rode my bicycle to town to go to the picture show. I wanted to get away from my terrible home life, and I knew a girl who would be there.

I had a crush on her because we always sat beside each other in school. Her name was Tiny B. We held hands in the show a few times so I was sure she was my girlfriend. But after I paid for my ticket and walked down to where we sat, she was there sitting with another boy.

I felt rejected so I turned around and left the movie. I got back on my bicycle and rode to the schoolhouse. I sat in a swing crying, telling God that no one loved me so please let me die.

It was about midnight when I left the school

thinking that since Hal had joined the army and was stationed at Fort Jackson in Columbia, South Carolina, that I'd run away and thumb a ride to be with him. But then I came upon a car lot and rode my bike in. I went through every car to see if I could find one with the keys in it. Having no luck finding a car I could steal, I started to leave feeling more disappointed.

Just as I started to leave, I spotted a wrecker truck at the side of the garage so I put my bike down, and looked in the truck. I could hardly believe it, in its ignition was a key, so I got in and drove off the lot heading for Florence. When I was younger Dad taught me to drive a stick shift car so I knew how to drive. It was dark and raining when I left Marion, but I managed to find the windshield wipers and lights after a few minutes.

Even though I was 14 years old, I was so short I could barely see over the dash of that old truck, and it's a wonder I didn't wreck it while driving that two-lane road at night in pouring down rain. But all I could think of was I'd finally be free from Clifton, my Dad, and maybe the aching I felt in my soul. I knew Hal would take care of me and show me the love I felt that I needed. I didn't know where he lived, but I knew was he was in the army in Columbia and I'd find him.

This was in the slow-paced '50s, and kids weren't as street-smart as they are today. Television was barely five years old with little or no violence. Girls and boys my age were embarrassed by the word sex and only held hands. If we did kiss it was only a lip touching and we had never heard of French kissing.

I was a naïve, hurting, abused kid in a stolen wrecker truck driving down a rain-soaked road thinking if I got to Columbia all the pain I felt would leave and I'd finally be happy. What I didn't know was that when I got to Florence my life would drastically change for the worse, and the happy feeling about Hal and my freedom would come to a screeching halt at a red light when the wrecker ran out of gas.

After it starting and dying several times, the battery finally died because the lights were still on. I didn't know it then but the God I had prayed to so many times in my pain was the one who protected me on that dark rainy night and allowed me to run out of gas at a well-lit intersection. After a few minutes a cop pulled up behind me and walked up to the truck. I'm sure when he opened the door he was confused when he saw a scrawny 4 ft. 10 in. boy who could barely see over the dash and looked to be around 10 or 11 years old. He said, "Son who's driving this truck?"

I said, "I am. I'm going to Columbia, South Carolina, to live with my brother who's in the army."

He said, "Whose truck is this?"

I lied and said, "It's my Daddy's."

He said, "Son, you're not old enough to be driving this truck, so come with me and I'll take you back home."

He lied so that I'd go with him. I got in the back of his police car and he drove to the police station. All the way there all I thought of was that he said he'd take me back home; and I had no intention of ever going back, so when he stopped to park in the alley behind the police station, I opened the back door and shot out between two store buildings, up a fire escape, and onto a roof. He didn't know where I went but he kept calling out, "Son, come on out. I won't hurt you. I'll feed you and I'll take care of you." I was soaked and cold from the drizzling rain so after a few more pleas from him I came down. He grabbed me by the collar and cussing at me said, "I oughta beat your butt for bringing me out in this rain."

I couldn't think of anything smart to say, so I replied, "You've got a coat on." He put me in a cell and I could hear him laughing as he told the desk officer about first seeing this little punk driving a stolen wrecker. I remember thinking if that fat old man knew how well I could sling these fists he wouldn't call me a punk. Being called a punk meant a law-breaking, rebellious smart-aleck juvenile delinquent. I finally warmed enough under that scratchy wool blanket to go to sleep. The next day a policeman from Marion came with the owner of the wrecker so he could take it back to his car lot, and he picked me up from the jail. He took me to the Marion County Jail and locked me in a cell by myself. I remember looking around to see all the writing people who'd been there before me had written on the walls. Around lunch time an old black man came on and asked me what did I want to eat for lunch. I asked him what did he have. He said, "Son, you came to the right place and here you can have anything you want to eat."

I said, "Can I have cheeseburgers and fries with lots of ketchup?"

He said, "You sure can. What do you want to drink?"

I asked, "What do you have?"

He said, "Do you like milkshakes?"

Being poor and never having been to a restaurant I thought I was about to eat some real fancy food with a milk shake, and it was like a dream come true. To me, things were looking up so I said, "Yes, I like milkshakes."

He asked, "Okay, what flavor do you want?"

I said, "What do you mean, what's a flavor?"

He said, "C'mon son, I haven't got all day. I've got to go next door to the Dairy Queen to get your cheeseburgers, fries and milkshake, so pick a flavor."

I still didn't know what a flavor was, so I said, "You pick me a flavor."

He said, "Well, kids like you who come in here for stealing cars or trucks always like chocolate, so I'll get you a chocolate milkshake, okay?" and he left. I savored the feeling of eating food only rich kids ate; that fantasy came to an end when two minutes later he walked up to my cell and put a metal tray on the perch. He laughed as he walked away. On the tray were cold grits with no seasoning, a hard biscuit and a small piece of slab bacon. I ate the biscuit and bacon.

That afternoon the jailer came and opened my cell and said, "Let's go, truck driver, your ride's here." I followed him to the front where Dad and Mom were waiting for me. I was actually glad to see them, and Mom hugged me. She asked, "Jimmy, what's gotten into you, son?"

I didn't answer her, but I asked, "Is Daddy mad? Is he gonna whip me?"

She said, "No, he wants to talk to you." That shocked me because Daddy never just talked to me, I didn't know what to expect.

When we got to the car, I got into the back seat behind Mom so I'd be out of Dad's reach. He turned around and said, "I went to Mr. Blair who owns the wrecker, and he agreed not to press charges if you go by and apologize to him and he's got your bicycle; so, if you want it, go see Mr. Blair."

He started the car and that was that. He never said another word about it until a few days later when I rode up on my bicycle. He said, "You talked to Mr. Blair?"

I said, "Yes, sir, he's a good man." Actually, I just saw my bike beside his office and no one was in but a lady at a desk so I just took my bike and rode away. I didn't care what happened to me anymore. I felt so unloved, unwanted, and lost on a heartless road. Before a year would pass, I would sink deeper into sin with what felt like no way out.

Soon school started, but I had lost interest. I wasn't learning anything, and by now all the smart kids, the rich kids, and the teachers acted like I had a disease when I had to get near them. I was assigned a desk at the back of the class close to other uninterested boys, so we talked during class. One boy named Jimmy B. and I became friends, and we made plans to cut school the next day to go to one of his favorite fishing holes.

CHAPTER 3

Next door to where we lived on Pine Street was a
family who had two older boys and one was in my
class that year. His name was Ronald M. I liked him
from the first, and it was Ronald who taught me to
smoke. He would buy a pouch of Tops tobacco and
roll his own cigarettes. I had seen this done on cowboy
shows at the movies, and I thought it was so cool so I
started rolling my own cigs. My dad caught me
smoking one day, but I caught him drinking a beer.
He had promised my mom he wouldn't drink
anymore. I sat down at the table across from him,
pulled out a cigarette and lit it up. He said, "What are
you doing with that?"

I said, "What are you doing with that beer?"

He said, "Okay, you can smoke, just keep it
between you and me."

So, all my friends smoked and rejected authority,
except Jimmy B. His mom and dad were very strict
and went to church all the time. I hadn't been to a

church in years, and I was heading towards bigger sins every day.

By now, cigarettes and beer couldn't fix that yearning in my soul. I was crying out to God for deliverance, but the path I was on wasn't one that led to Him. A couple of my friends' Dad was an alcoholic, and he drank moonshine until he passed out. They would help him to bed, but then rob him of all his money. We'd buy a case of beer and get drunk. Nobody told us we were wrong, so I just learned to sin, I had no boundaries.

Jimmy B. and I cut school a lot, and he started acting like me. My life was about to take another drastic change because trying to be cool to impress another kid will lead to wrong.

One day I talked Jimmy into cutting school. We rode our bicycles on the back-country roads so nobody would see us. His parents didn't want him hanging around with me, because they saw I was troubled. When Jimmy told me what his mom had said, I thought, "I'm not a troubled kid. I'm just trying to find my way." I already believed no one, including God, loved me, so I didn't care. He told me his mom said she was praying for me.

As Jimmy and I rode our bikes that day, we came upon the plant where my mom and dad worked, called American Wood Products. It was on the outskirts of Marion. I parked my bike and started looking through the cars for a key in the ignition. I soon found an old '51 Chevrolet. After a little coaxing Jimmy jumped in and I drove off. Even though I was still 14 years old, I'd grown a little, so this time I could see over the dash.

I drove around Marion then headed to the North Carolina border. Jimmy listened as I told him how we'd get a job, and live with no parents or mean brothers like Clifton. It was Clifton I was running away from. Even though the beatings had stopped, he was still verbally abusive. Jimmy had an aunt in Ellerbe, a little town in North Carolina, so we headed there.

When we got to the city limits, we parked at a sawmill on the edge of town and walked from there. We made up a story that we thumbed a ride and wanted to find jobs so we could get a place to live.

She was smarter than we realized because she called Jimmy's mom who told her a car was stolen from the plant. They were sure Jimmy was with me and that I stole the car. She called the police who took us to jail where they put us in different cells so we couldn't talk to each other.

When they brought me out to talk, they said Jimmy had already told on me, and asked where was the car. I told him everything. Then they put us together. I started fussing with Jimmy about telling on me. He said that the police had told him the same thing so he thought I had confessed and he also told him where the car was.

When the Marion Police Department took us back, I was put in jail but Jimmy wasn't. His parents put all the blame on me to get him off. Actually, they had every right to, because I had persuaded him the whole time.

A few days after that, I found myself in the Florence Juvenile Boys' Home. It was there I had my second experience with God. Once there, I was assigned to an old building named Pickens Unit.

The office staff took a boy's stature and age into consideration; and because I was very short for a 14-year-old, only 4 ft. 11, I was assigned to a building where most of the boys were around 12 years of age. This helped me survive for the next year that I was there.

I had fought off my brother's homosexual attacks so I knew how bigger boys tried to molest smaller ones, and now I was forced to live where homosexual acts were the norm. Everywhere you looked boys were touching other boys right under the staff's noses. At night, many boys passed my bed crawling on hands and knees to get into bed with another boy. I was propositioned all the time by boys with sodas or candy. But even though I knew nothing of the Bible's stand against homosexuality something inside me didn't like it. I was attracted to the opposite sex.

For work detail, I was assigned to the garden crew. South Carolina Industrial School was wholly self-sufficient by growing their own food to eat. All their eggs, chicken and milk came from the farm as did the hogs and beef that were raised on the corn they grew. I've never worked so hard before this, but because of it my body began to change. I no longer smoked because it wasn't allowed. I didn't stay up late at night anymore because after hoeing fields and fields of beans, potatoes and tomatoes from sun up to sun down, I had blisters on top of blisters the first two weeks I was there. After I showered, all I wanted was to go to bed.

The weekends were full of fun and games. We had a school and gym, and attended church on the weekends. After a few weeks passed, one weekend day we went to the rec field. The coach asked us to team up and to play a game of baseball against his hand-picked institutional team so they could get some practice. They played against local Little League teams and Pony League squads, and this was a serious coach who wanted to win. They had a near perfect record and he wanted to keep it that way. He also was the coach of the boxing team.

As yet I hadn't told him about my history with the Golden Glove. So, we teamed up with other boys in our age bracket. As I watched the boys who played their regular positions, the coach asked me if I could play baseball. I told him that I was a pitcher or an outfielder so he sent me to right field. Any kid who has ever played baseball knows that right field doesn't see much action and normally the worst player gets put there just so he gets to play.

The pitcher on my team walked the first three batters, and a line drive over the center fielder's head drove all three runners in with the cleanup batter on third. I started getting aggravated because I knew I could do better. Finally, we got three outs and they had seven runs in the first inning.

When we went in to bat, I told our pitcher, "If you can't throw a strike why don't you sit down." He got mad and pushed me, so I put up my fists and gave him a few of my choicest cuss words. He came at me swinging. I punched and counter punched him into quick submission.

The coach grabbed my shirt collar and spun me around. Letting go of my shirt he said, "If you can pitch as good as you fight not only will I try you out on our boxing team, but I'll give you a spot on the baseball team."

When we went back out, I walked to the mound and warmed up. My catcher's name was Mike K. After a few fast, straight throws, Mike, who was a good catcher, knew a good pitcher was up. Wherever he put his mitt for target I hit or was close enough that it was a strike. Because of the seven-run lead they had we lost, but I was making a statement.

The ball and boxing teams ate better, were treated and trained better so I was given a jersey. We played against some good teams that year. I kept noticing a kid who looked familiar. He was third baseman, and a few days after our first game he came over to me and told me I looked familiar to him. When he asked me where I was from, I told him I was from Marion. He said he fought the toughest fight he'd ever been in with a left-handed kid from Marion named Jimmy Windham. I almost couldn't believe my ears, for in front of me stood the kid who made me hate losing and who caused me to train harder. I said, "Are you Dexter C.?"

He said, "Yes."

I said, "I'm Jimmy Windham."

We went on to be the best friends and never had to fight each other because of being on the same boxing team, but we sparred a few times; and I was proud when Dexter, who also had a brother there named Danny, told me one day, "I'm glad I don't have to fight you again, because I hate to lose."

When baseball season was over, we started training for the boxing team. Our coach was an old Marine jarhead who had been a drill sergeant, and he brought all his military training to our school. After a week or two he made me wish I was working back in the garden; but with all the miles we ran, the calisthenics and the gym bags we punched, when I got in the ring, I knew then why I had lost my first fight to Dexter.

CHAPTER 4

Visiting day was the last Sunday of the month, and Mom, Dad and Carolyn would go to church with me. I must have been growing because I noticed Carolyn was getting shorter every time I saw her.

However, the emptiness I felt was still there, and sometimes at night I'd lay in bed and cry myself to sleep feeling like no one loved me. But one particular morning in church the pastor preached about love. He said, "Most of you boys are here because you came from broken homes and you haven't been loved." He went on to preach a message similar to the first one I had heard by the old preacher in Ridgeland, South Carolina, about needing a Savior named Jesus Christ. It seemed to be directed towards me and I felt convicted of my sins so I wept a lot. I was a jock so I didn't care what anybody thought. I only knew I wanted to be loved, and at that moment I wanted God to love me.

When he gave the altar call and said, "If you'll come

to this altar God will forgive you of your sins and put His Holy Spirit in you," I went to the altar; and with tears running down my face I repented before God for all my sins. I can't explain what I felt and I know that faith isn't "feeling," but it felt like a hundred pounds had been lifted off my shoulders. I felt different and I felt loved. It seemed everything changed. The music sounded prettier and the sky looked bluer.

Those of us who went forward were asked to memorize a few Bible verses to quote the next weekend. Mine was John 1:1-14. To this day I can still quote that passage.

I won a Bible for learning scripture, and I began to read it. I even began talking to God because now I believed He was listening.

Shortly afterwards my year was up so I went back home. I soon forgot God and the Bible because I went back to the same life I ran away from and hung out with the same old friends and fell back into the same old ways. I got a job, though, at a body shop sanding down cars so I could buy cigarettes and weekend beer.

Right after I left the boys' home Mom and Dad separated and never lived together again. Daddy left us, moved to Florence, met a woman named Doris and they moved to Florida to be near her family. Mama moved us to an upstairs apartment in a two-story plantation-looking house which had magnolia trees in the front yard. Moss grew abundantly in Marion and the street light filtering through all the moss felt eerie.

I had turned 15 by now. Mr. Smith, who sold groceries and beer in his small store, lived nearby. He had a couple of pinball machines that paid a nickel for each game you won. I spent a lot of time in there playing pinball with the other guys who went there to drink beer.

My brother Hal had come home from the army and had gotten married. Clifton also had married a girl named Pat from Thomasville, North Carolina. They had a small apartment above Mama's apartment. By now I had gotten as tall as Clifton, but I was muscled up while he was slightly fat and chunky. He still had a habit of talking down to me, and I was still intimidated by his attitude.

CHAPTER 5

Dad's brother came to Mama's house while I was gone and told her that Daddy wanted me to come to Florida to live with him. When I left the boys' home I was put on a year's probation; so Mama told him that I couldn't go until my probation was over. When it was up, she'd ask if I wanted to go live with him.

I was in the eighth grade now and one of the requirements of probation was that I had to stay in school, make passing grades, and stay out of trouble. It wasn't hard to do because I made up my mind when I left the boys' home that I'd never go back. Second-time offenders had to stay until they turned 18. The day my parents picked me up, I told my friends they wouldn't ever see me again. I meant it because I didn't like being controlled and at the school they had total control.

Shortly before I left there, though, one day during lunch, I looked over at the Kershaw Cottage and there sat my friend Jimmy B. from Marion, the boy I'd persuaded to steal the car at the plant where my parents worked. We weren't allowed to talk in the chow hall or in line going to and from anywhere so I couldn't talk to him. To this day, I've never seen him again. When I got back to Marion, I asked my friends why he had to go to SCIS and was told he had stolen a car. This time his parents couldn't blame me. I can only hope and pray that he found his way back.

Once home, Hal and I rarely saw each other since he lived across town with his wife. Clifton and his wife Pat worked at the same textile mill so our paths crossed only on weekends. Carolyn was still in school, and when she came home, she and Mama cooked supper, then go to their room to relax and watch TV. I still felt alone and it seemed the only way to lose that longing in my soul was to get drunk.

I loved to play pinball and had gotten really good at not tilting the machine so I won a lot more than I lost. When I won, I used my winnings to buy Schlitz malt liquor which I drank. If I was out of money, the older men would ask me to play for them, and we'd use whatever I won to buy beer, plus they'd also buy beers while I played. My life consisted of going to school only because I had to and coming home to an empty house. By "empty" I mean I didn't fit in or feel loved. Everyone but me seemed to have a life.

One day after I had gotten out of school for the weekend, I went to Mr. Smith's store and the evening turned to night as I drank, smoked and played pinball. When I came home that night, I went out on our upstairs balcony; I looked up and said, "God I know you're real." I started crying and said, "There has to be more to life than this."

Instantly I felt as if 1,000 volts of electricity went through my body. With my arms raised towards heaven, I cried and repented for all my sins. Again, I felt as though 100 pounds had left my shoulders. I felt peace and love surround me and in my very soul. I ran in the house yelling, "Mama, Mama!" She and Carolyn came out of her bedroom to find out why I was yelling.

She said, "Jimmy, what's wrong with you, son."

I said, "Mama, Jesus just saved me!" I was still crying and so happy.

She said, "Jimmy, go to bed. You're drunk, you don't need to be playing with God this way."

Isn't it always like that, when God does something good for someone who is beat down by sin, Satan is right there to steal it? This was a real experience with God which sobered me up, but Mama could smell the beer on my breath and convinced me I was wrong so I went to bed. I soon forgot that experience and returned to my old ways, but I've never forgotten that wonderful feeling.

My dad had bought me a nice gold Elgin 21-jewel watch when I left the boys' home and it was the only possession I had, and I was so proud of it. One Saturday morning Clifton asked if he could wear it. I finally gave in. I left for work, but all day I had a gut feeling that I had made a big mistake letting him take my watch. I kept hoping I was wrong.

When I got home that evening he wasn't there. I went to his apartment to check if he was home. His wife said he had left around noon when a few of his work buddies came by to see if he wanted to go bowling at Florence. Because she didn't go bowling with him, I knew they weren't out bowling. I asked Pat to tell him when he got home to bring my watch to me. She said she would.

I was sitting in the living room watching TV while Mama and Carolyn sat in the kitchen talking when Clifton came walking into the room. He had a plastic cup in his hand which smelled of strong whiskey so I knew he was about drunk. Usually I'd stay seated when he got near me but I stood up because he wasn't wearing my watch. I asked him, "Where's my watch, Clifton?"

He was within arm's reach of me. He sneered at me and said, "I sold it, little boy, and if you don't like it do something about it."

I said, "You know, Clifton, all my life I've taken your crap but tonight I'm giving it back." I punched him so hard and fast he couldn't recover. Blood poured from his nose and lips as I repeatedly punched him. He tried to grab me but couldn't because I was upper cutting him in his face and stomach. He was no match for me.

All the years of training was for that one night. I believe every time I stepped into a ring, I had been fighting him. I had been so scared of him because, psychologically, he controlled me. Just one of his sneers sent chills up my spine. His taunting made me shiver, and until this night when I called his bluff, he thought he could always taunt me.

I stopped punching and stood there while he staggered back and forth. It was over! Mom came running in when it was almost over but couldn't jump in for fear of getting hurt herself. But she grabbed him and looked at me and screamed, "Just look at what you've done to your brother. I hope you're happy now."

Carolyn stood in the kitchen doorway and Pat, who had heard the noise of the fight, came running in. She went to the bathroom where Mama was cleaning Clifton. She came back out, walked over to me and slapped me hard twice. Carolyn went to the kitchen to fill an ice pack to put on Clifton's face as I stood there alone.

Am I proud that I had beaten my older brother?

Now, I say no, I'm sorry it came to that. No one but me knew how I felt that night when he had sold my watch. I felt he had sold me and any compassion I'd ever had for him. Afterwards I saw all he had were words full of evil. But then, I saw a mixed-up terrified child who had only known violence and evil, because he had no father figure and no discipline or Godly leadership in his life. Today I'm so sorry I hurt my brother.

He was a mama's boy. But maybe Mama saw what I couldn't. She saw her little mixed up boy so she tried to love him straight. Maybe she saw me as a loner who she knew one day would find the way even if I had to do it alone. Clifton's dead now. He died in prison 30 days before he was supposed to max out a 25-year sentence. But he didn't die alone. His mother was there with her baby and his last words to her were, "Mama, will Jesus forgive any sin?"

She said, "Yes, son, He'll forgive any sin if we ask Him."

He closed his eyes in death and said, "Well, I'm forgiven."

Oh, to die forgiven is a treasure from a loving God. Just one drop of that precious blood can make the vilest sinner clean. But I had a long way to go before I met the One who can straighten out any sinner's crooked path.

CHAPTER 6

After I beat up Clifton, Mama went to my probation officer and told him that Dad wanted me to live with him in Florida, and she was moving to North Carolina where her family lived. She convinced him that I had straightened up and needed no supervision, so he agreed to let me off probation early. She then asked my uncle to call my dad to see if he still wanted me. He did, so my uncle took me to the bus station and bought a ticket to Belle Glade, Florida, where dad lived with his new wife, Doris, and her son Jerry.

Dad had been on the police force a few times, so getting a job at Glades Correctional Institution was right up his alley. He had a good job, a nice little bungalow in a good section of town with an instant family; but he was lonely, and though I hadn't asked to come, it felt good to know he sent for me.

Across the street from our house was the swimming pool where kids and teenagers came to swim and hang out. I was now a cute 16-year-old blond, blue-eyed kid who was in heaven. I became friends with the popular kids because of Dad's new station in life. They were policemen, highway patrolmen, a doctor who worked at Belle Glade Correctional Institute, prison guards, and local businessmen.

Doris's daughter was married to the army recruiter who ran the VFW that was in the National Guard Armory. My friends and I were always invited to the parties there. My drinking became worse because of the parties every week, and my friends and I would sneak cases of beer from the armory's cooler. No one seemed to notice or care because I was family and went wherever I wanted. My friends and I partied all the time.

This was all new for me, because where I had come from, I was always alone and $25 that I earned from working all week was big money. Now I had money handed to me from Dad's new family and friends.

Lake Okeechobee was a mere 20-minute drive from Belle Glade, so some days I fished all day with the other boys while pretty girls in bathing suits sat next to me. The lake that had so many fish in it you'd almost have to hide behind a tree to bait your hook.

I drove one of the hottest cars in town, a beautiful white '55 Pontiac with red leather interior and a radio that blasted music. Dad wanted to be my friend and encouraged my new lifestyle of parties, girls, friends and drinking, but inside my heart I still wasn't happy. I longed for something to fill that gap but I didn't know what it was that was missing.

One day at the pool I met a pretty girl named Cathy. I hadn't seen her before so I introduced myself. She told me she'd seen me around but since I hung out with the popular crowd, she hadn't yet talked to me. I told her, "But I'm really not one of them."

She said, "You had me fooled. So, if you're not

really one of them, give me a ride home."

I said, "Sure." We walked across the street to my dad's house so I could change. She and her brother had changed at the pool. I invited them in and gave them a soda as I went to change.

Dad and Doris had a nice home with comfortable furnishings. I was used to that because my mom was a hard worker all her life and always dressed us and kept nice furnishings, but this girl kept telling me that our house was beautiful.

Once I drove them home, I knew why. She lived in a poor area in an old wood-frame house. But when I was invited in to meet her family, I saw something I'd never felt before. Her mom and dad asked her how was her day as they smiled ear to ear and listened.

When we first walked in, they hugged their kids like they'd been gone for a week. I saw love and knew it was what I had always wanted all my life. After she and her brother excitedly told all about their pool day their mom began to ask me questions about myself, so I shared the basic stuff of who I was, where I was from, who my dad was, and where I lived. They thanked me for bringing their daughter and son home and invited me back sometime.

Cathy walked with me to the car and thanked me again, and then she asked, "You said you weren't really one of the in-crowd kids that I see you hanging around with, so can I invite you to go with me to our church Sunday morning?"

I told her to let me think about it and if she'd give me her phone number, I'd call her to let her know. I had no plans to go to church because I was having too much fun but Cathy was so different.

Up until then I don't remember even having kissed a girl, and now girls were wanting me to go everywhere with them. She gave me her number on a matchbook cover I had in my car and I left. All week even though I was with my other friends I couldn't get Cathy out of my mind so I called her. We talked for a while, then she asked me had I thought about going to church with her so I told her that I hadn't made up my mind. I really had no intention of going but I liked her and I finally told her I would go.

That Sunday morning, I picked her and her brother up at her house and she told me how to get to their church. As we were driving into the parking lot, I saw the church sign on the front lawn and the name, Bella Glade Church of God. I thought to myself, "Uh oh!" When I was a kid my dad took me to the Church of God, and once he started going, he stopped drinking beer, smoking, and beating my mama. I told myself this is the first and last church visit with her.

The church was an old wood-frame building that had wooden benches with no padding in the seats. Everybody was hugging and shaking hands and so friendly to each other; I didn't know how to act so I slid into a bench on the back row and sat down. In a little while Cathy came back to me and asked me if I'd like to sit with her so I asked, "Where?"

She said, "On the front row." I told her no, I was okay where I was. Truth was, I wanted to watch them and I couldn't if I was sitting up front. Cathy slid in beside me because, I think, she didn't want me to leave early. We went to Sunday school classes, then came back to sit a few benches from the back. They had guitars, drums, a piano, and people beating on tambourines while they sang lively songs with people raising their hands and praising the Lord. It wasn't so much that these church people were so friendly as much as it was that I knew it was truly God's clean Holy Spirit that I was feeling. I had felt His Spirit around me before.

I kept watching Cathy out of the corner of my eye, and her right hand was up above her head. She was mumbling words I couldn't understand, and tears were streaming down her face. Whatever she had was causing emotions within her. I also was experiencing a strange feeling but I felt unworthy to respond to this Spirit.

As Cathy and the others in unison began standing up and praising their God, I also stood up so I wouldn't be different. She and others were speaking in a language I had heard as a kid in that small tabernacle across the road from my house. Then something else happened. A little child began to interpret a message to the congregation. She said, "From a little child I placed my hand on you and I've led you to me many times in your life as my protective hand was upon you. The enemy of your soul has come many times as a roaring lion to destroy you, but your guardian angel drove him back because I love you. Seek my face and I'll be found by you, for the Lord has spoken this." Cathy reached over and placed her hand on mine and I instantly felt light again.

Now, I can tell you that even though I felt conviction and I felt like running out of there, I just stood there. I knew inside me that no child could've made this up, because, for one thing, she didn't know I was there. I began to reason it away thinking if this was the Lord speaking, He wasn't talking to me. I wanted to go home, drink a beer, smoke a cigarette, and forget about church.

The pastor stood up and said, "If there's someone here who wants us to pray for them come forward now." A few people went forward so I told myself I wasn't the one who needed prayer. I was glad when, after a few up-tempo songs, a sermon by the pastor and people standing up telling about how good their

God had been to them all week, we were dismissed.

As I drove Cathy and her brother back to their home we didn't speak much. I was deep in thought about what had just happened. I was going over and over in my head what that little girl had said because it was something I couldn't take lightly. I knew I believed in God but I also knew I wasn't ready to give up my new-found lifestyle. I was finally being accepted by my dad, his friends and family and living a teenager's dream. Once we parked outside of Cathy's home, she asked me to come in and eat dinner with them. But I made up some lame excuse for not coming in. She said, "I won't see you again, will I?"

I shrugged it off by saying, "Sure you will. I go to the pool almost every day."

Before she got out of my dad's car she leaned over and kissed me on my cheek and said, "Jimmy Windham, Jesus loves you and He died for you." She left. She had mentioned that her mom sent her and her kid brother to the pool only on Wednesdays because she was off from work that day. From then on, I went fishing on Wednesdays.

CHAPTER 7

A few days after I dropped Cathy at her house, I saw a dead person for the first time and it started me thinking about what would happen if I died. A bus load of people, who worked on one of the sugar cane farms in the area, ran off the road into a moat beside the highway and they all drowned. After a wrecker pulled the bus out of the water, the bodies were taken to the National Guard Armory where they were laid on the floor in a line. Because my stepmom's son-in-law was the sergeant who ran the armory I was allowed inside. As I viewed their swollen bodies, I restrained myself for a few days. I knew God and death were real and I was afraid of both.

Shortly after this I came home one day and found again my life was about to dramatically change. I had been out with a few of my friends fishing from a bridge. After we had caught our fish, cleaned and cooked them, we ate and drank beer. Then we went back onto the bridge which was high above the lake and began showing off by diving. At that point, a teenage boy who came from a small town in South Carolina couldn't ask for a better life. We finished our beers and I left for home.

When I walked into our living room my dad and Doris were sitting there with a sad look on their faces. Daddy asked me to sit down. My new life and all the fun I had been experiencing for the past six months was about to end. Dad said, "Son, I know that what I'm about to tell you isn't something you want to hear, but Doris and I have decided to go back to Florence at the end of this month." They had already made up their minds and never asked me my opinion. He said his brother already had a house on Pine Street rented and waiting and he'd be here to rent a U-Haul to help them move.

I yelled, "You can't do this to me! I have friends here, and I finally fit in somewhere. You never even asked what I wanted!" and I ran out of the room.

He followed and told me that I could still live with him and Doris in Florence if I wanted. When Daddy left the room my anger for him began to rage in me because I blamed him for destroying my new life.

My mom and Carolyn had moved to Thomasville, North Carolina, with Clifton and his wife, Pat, and I'd had no contact with her, but she was still my mom. I called directory assistance in Thomasville and got my mom's phone number. I waited until that afternoon to call. When she finally got home, I cried as I told her what Daddy was doing and I asked if I could live with her. At first, she gave me a few excuses why she didn't think it would be a good idea for me and Clifton to live together in the same house, but she asked me to call her back in an hour.

When I called, Clifton answered the phone. He said, "Listen you little bastard, you broke my nose that night I was drunk and one day I'll get even with you. But Mom said you can come here on two conditions. One, you have to go back to school. (I had quit when I turned 16), and two, you have to get an after-school job to pay your room and board."

I told him, "Clifton, I'm sorry I hit you and I accept those conditions."

He said, "Yeah, whatever, see you soon," and hung up. I went into the living room where Dad and Doris were watching TV and I told them that I wasn't going to Florence with them because I decided to go to live with Mom in North Carolina. They tried to talk me out of my decision with my dad even telling me he'd give me the Pontiac if I'd go with them. That should've been an easy decision but I know now that I had a pre-ordained destiny awaiting me in North Carolina arranged by the true and living God!

I had already called the Trailways Bus Station in Belle Glade to find out when a bus would leave for Thomasville and was told one left at 10 the next morning. I told Dad my plans and he reluctantly agreed to take me there the next morning.

That night I thought of all I was leaving and one by one I called my friends to tell them I wouldn't see them again. Then I called Cathy. I really felt embarrassed to call her but she sounded happy when she answered until I told her my plans. She softly cried as she told me that she had been praying for me and she believed that God had His hand on me and one day I wouldn't be able to run from God anymore. I didn't see it that way, but I listened. When we hung up, she was still crying. At that time, I couldn't figure out why because I thought she should have been mad at me for dumping her. I know now that it was her love for God and a lost soul that made her ask me to go to church with her and not because I was a teenage boy. She was a true born-again Christian as was her family and that's why I had felt so uncomfortable around her.

I was nearing my 17th birthday and my life had already been full of changes and now here I was about to go into another one. I had no foundation under me and it shouldn't be that way in a child's life. It seemed that every two years or so I was uprooted and that added to my insecurities and confusion.

The next morning Dad and Doris took me to the bus station in Belle Glade to board a bus for Thomasville. Dad took me inside, bought my ticket, bought me four packs of my favorite cigarettes, and gave me $20 for eating. When my bus arrived and, before I boarded, they hugged me told me if I changed my mind, I could come to Florence to live with them. At that time, I had no intention of living with them again because I was so disappointed in my dad for causing me to have to leave a life I loved. While I lived in Florida, I seemed to have lost the emptiness and loneliness that I had lived with all my life, and as I sat on that bus it all came back and I blamed my dad for it. I also began to think about what Clifton had said to me, and having grown up with his violence I knew when he said, "I'll get even with you," he was already plotting revenge. I kept going back over that night I had won our first real fight and wondering if he had been sober would it have been the other way around. I laid my seat back and let myself drift off into sleep. From years of experience, I already had a way to quickly forget where I had been and to just let whatever came just come.

When I arrived in Thomasville the next day my mom, Carolyn, Clifton, and Pat were waiting for me at the bus station. Mama drove me all around the town showing me the sights. I noticed they had a skating rink, a swimming pool, a downtown theatre, and the biggest chair in the world sitting on Main Street. I asked Mom to stop to let me see the chair. I asked her why they built a chair so big that no one in town could sit in it, and she laughed but told me that Thomasville was a furniture-producing town with many factories called "Finch's Chairs." Then she drove me over to an adjoining town called High Point where she worked at a plant called Alma Desk Company.

Shortly after arriving at my new home I made good on Mama's first request when I enrolled in the ninth grade at school. I should've been in the 11th, but because I kept having to take grades over, I was put in the ninth grade. I felt uncomfortable being a few months from my 17th birthday and in classes with 14-year-olds, so after two weeks I quit again. I had begun going to the theatre and skating rink because that's where all the teenagers hung out.

CHAPTER 8

Elvis Presley was the American teen idol at that time, and all the teenage boys (except the "preppies") wanted to look and sing like him. I was always a towhead (blond) but I dyed my hair black, bought a black leather jacket, and got a job at the theater as an usher and filling the drink and candy machines It allowed me to sit beside a pretty girl every night. My life was looking up.

Elvis's movies were showing all the time and I soon found that I could sing like him. When he sang on the set, I sang along with him which made the girls swoon over me. I was too young to own a car so I put a down payment on a new bicycle and made payments. Because I was taking care of myself, Mom and I were getting along. Mama's mother lived nearby with my Uncle Carlyle, and Mama's sister Gen, along with her husband Scarborough, and daughter Shirley, lived not far from us.

Clifton seemed to be enjoying life because he and

Pat had a baby boy named Keith. He was working at a furniture factory in Thomasville. Clifton was always a good dresser so he had nice pants and shirts to wear. I wore blue jeans and a T-shirt with a pack of cigarettes rolled up in my sleeve because that was the way Elvis, James Dean and the cool kids wore their clothes.

One night as I started to leave for work Clifton started talking down to me. At first, I thought maybe this is the night he finally wants to fight but he fooled me. He said, "When are you going to stop dressing like a teenage rebel and dress nice for a change?"

I said, "I'm dressed for work." He and I were about the same size except that he was about an inch taller than me.

He said "Come to my bedroom." Still a little unsure of what he had in mind I followed him anyway. Once in his and Pat's room he opened the closet, pulled out one of his beautiful blue paisley shirts, a pair of dark black slacks, a pair of his oxford penny loafers and out of a dresser drawer he got out a pair of blue socks. He said, "These will show off your blue eyes and maybe you'll finally get you 'some' because I know you're still a virgin."

I said, blushing, "Am not!" though, really, I was.

Then he floored me! No, not with his fist, but with his words. He said, "I know this won't make up for your watch I sold but it's a start." And then he hugged me. Right at that moment that was the greatest few minutes we had ever shared.

I left for the theater. I have to admit that being dressed like that was different for me and a lot of my friends at the theatre asked me where had I gone to before coming to the theater? One of the girls said, "Jimmy, you look like my dad. Where's your leather jacket?"

If some of you've ever watched the show *Happy*

Days, well that character Fonzie took that look from us. James Dean was the original, then Elvis started out for a while in the early '50s with it until he got popular. But we boys kept that look until around '63.

One night I was filling the soda machine with cups, syrup, and caramel cola and I turned around to see a pretty girl was looking at me. It was love at first sight (literally). We didn't say a word for about a minute it seemed until I finally asked, "Would you like a soda?"

She said, "Yes, but I'll wait until you're through." I closed the machine, dropped a dime and a nickel in it, and bought her a coke.

We just stood there looking at each other until I said, "Would you like to sit down? My name is Jimmy."

She said, "My name is Mildred." We sat down and talked, and for the next six months we were inseparable. She was my first love and I was hers. I began going to her house and sat on her porch swing where we talked for hours while her dad, Charlie, was at work. She, like me, wasn't a churchgoer but we sometimes talked about God. Her mom liked me.

Then she introduced me to her dad. After I left, he threw a fit and told her she was "never to see that little hoodlum again." She was my first love and had given herself to me and now we were told we were never to see each other again.

My world stopped. I was 17 and she was 15 so we did what all teenagers do. We outsmarted him. She and I had a mutual friend who lived near her and he would go over to her house and ask Charlie could Mildred go skating or to the theater with him. Charlie was glad to let her go with him and would drop them off. They'd go in and she'd sit with me. He'd drop her off at the skating rink and we'd dance skate together.

I had plans to marry Mildred when she turned 18

so when Mama asked me if I wanted to go back home with her, I turned her down and moved in with my uncle, who took me to work every morning, then on weekends I'd meet Mildred somewhere. We were already sexually active with only each other and in love so we were waiting for the day we could get married. We knew nothing of God's laws about fornication. Actually, I was living like most people live, do whatever seems right in your own knowledge and if it isn't hurting anyone it can't be wrong.

When I turned 17, I quit the theater and I went to the Finch's Chair Company's main office to see about a job. Clifton had told me to tell them I was 18 so I put my birthday back a year on my application. My life was about to change again because the God I didn't know had led me to North Carolina for two reasons. One, to meet Him for my first time and two, my precious first child Jennifer would be born there a year and a half later.

I was hired at one of the factories making dressers. Mom moved back to Marion shortly after that so I moved in with my Uncle Carlyle. Though all my mama's relatives were good hardworking moral people, none of them ever went to church or mentioned faith in God. So now with Mama, Carolyn, Clifton, and Pat gone I was alone again.

Shortly after I was hired at Finch's, Charlie picked Mildred up in the parking lot of the bowling alley. I had waited inside for about 15 minutes to give them time to leave but Charlie ran into a friend who was picking up her kid there. I walked out and they all were standing there. When Charlie saw me, he instantly knew that he had been duped. He asked Mildred, "How long have you been sneaking around with him?"

She said, "But Daddy, I love him." He told her to go

get in the car. He looked at me and said, "I told you to stay away from my daughter."

I said, "But why? What have I done to you?"

His words cut hard and deep. He said, "Because you're trash and you won't ever amount to anything but a hoodlum. Stay away from her." Charlie's oldest daughter had run away from home and wouldn't have anything to do with him. Charlie's wife killed herself while Mildred and I were together, and now Mildred was like a prisoner in her home. She couldn't talk on the phone, Charlie's sister drove Mildred to school, picked her up, and sat with her until he got home from work. He worked the second shift at a textile mill so Mildred had round-the-clock supervision. I couldn't see her, talk to her, or find any way to get a message to her. This whole thing made me feel like I was going crazy.

One day I tried calling again and since it had been months since we had talked or seen each other I was surprised when Mildred answered the phone. I couldn't believe what she had to say. After we said hello, she said, "Listen, Jimmy, my dad's right. We're too young to know what we want so I started seeing another boy and I don't want you to call me anymore." I was shocked and pleaded with her not to give up on us or me. She coldly said, "Look, Jimmy, don't call me anymore," and hung up.

For the next two weeks, I couldn't think of anything else but her daddy's words and that she said "my daddy's right." I couldn't sleep, I couldn't eat, I was so depressed. My uncle took me to work each morning but I couldn't concentrate on anything. When I came home from work that evening all I could think of was taking my own life. I went into the bathroom to find a razor to cut my wrist. I didn't find a razor, but I found a bottle of aspirin. Mildred's mama took her life by taking a bottle of pills so I believed Mildred would understand I did it for her because I couldn't live without her love.

I took the whole bottle and laid on my bed as I waited to die. All night long I laid there hearing a loud buzz in my ears. I didn't die but I jokingly say that a headache wouldn't come within a mile of me that night. I got up the next morning and went to work.

A few days earlier, one of the men I worked with invited me to a revival at his church. I asked him what kind of church, because I knew there were a few that had a spirit that I didn't want to feel. Not because they weren't of God; but because they were! He said the Church of God. That was the one I was afraid to go to, because I always felt I needed to repent when I went. I told him, "Oh, no, I don't want to go."

Now bear in mind I had just tried to take my own life because I was love sick and needed Mildred. His next words got to me fast. He said, "Well, there's a lot of pretty young girls there." Before I fell for Mildred, I had a lot of girlfriends and being a kid, I enjoyed being a prize catch, and he just said "a lot" of pretty girls. I needed no further invitation.

He didn't have to try as a Christian to help get me saved by begging me to please come. I said, "What time will you pick me up?"

He said, "Around 6 or 6:30." I was waiting on him when he arrived.

If my memory serves me, his name was Todd, and I believe his wife was Naomi. He lived in an old wooden house next door to his mom and dad and he had some younger brothers. He left me there while he went home to dress. His brothers and I got acquainted. They were countrified and I'd like to think that because of the way I dressed they thought I was cool. So we cut up and laughed out on the front porch as I smoked and waited.

When we arrived at church, I sat on the back left row with his brothers who were still cutting up and laughing. I looked around and he was right, there were a lot of young ladies there who kept turning around in their seats to see who was coming in but before they turned back around, they smiled at me. When the service started, the choir was invited forward by the pastor named Bro. Crumpton. They had guitar players, drums, a piano, and the pastor's son, Ronnie, who later became my best friend. He played the meanest trumpet I had ever heard at that time. Later in life I heard and loved Phil Driscoll.

They started singing and, boy, could they sing! I could see by their faces that they were singing what was in their hearts. They sang "Oh I'm redeemed by love divine. Glory, glory, Christ is mine." With tears running down their faces, they raised their hands, and I knew I had done it again. I was back in God's holy presence and I couldn't run.

The brothers were used to this because they were raised in it, so they kept cutting up, but I kept my head down hoping God wouldn't see me. After the song service ended, they asked, "Does anyone have a testimony for the Lord?" A few stood up one at a time and told about a blessing God gave them during the week or maybe a miracle of healing. I could tell they meant it because they were so excited and would jump and shout. Some spoke in tongues.

(If you don't believe in a separate *gift* of tongues you haven't read your Bible! This book isn't meant to debate or indoctrinate anybody. It's meant only to point you to Christ. I'm not worthy to judge anybody but to God be the glory and my 34 years so far behind these bars is just a small sacrifice compared to what Christ did for all of us at Calvary's cruel cross.)

Anyway, the evangelist was from Lexington, North Carolina, Church of God. When he began to read the Scriptures from behind that pulpit he didn't stay there long because he got anointed by the Holy Spirit and walked up and down the aisles calling sin, sin. He also told of Jesus' blood, Jesus' resurrection and how to get rid of sin and death.

He gave an invitation to come forward to meet Jesus and get saved; I held on to the bench to keep from running to the front. I was glad when the service ended and I was introduced to the people there and, especially to the girls (the reason I went there). But God had a different reason that I'd soon understand. The next day at work I was under such strong conviction, and I kept wondering what if I died suddenly like that bus load of people who drowned in Florida. I literally got scared and, before the day was out, I asked Bro. Todd if was he going to church that night? He said, "Yes."

I said, "Please come by and pick me up because I want to go." This time it wasn't to see girls. I wanted to go because God was drawing me, I couldn't wait to go back. When we finally got there, I sat halfway toward the front, away from the distraction of his brothers; and that night as that evangelist preached, I knew that every word he was preaching about sin and death was to me. I cried all through his preaching and I couldn't wait for him to invite me forward. When he finally did, I ran to the right side of the two altars and put my face in the lap of Jesus, and I repented with all my heart. When I stood up and turned around, everyone was happy and smiling. The men who prayed with me hugged me and told me I was saved. The whole church had changed and become new. It was even brighter to me. I was now one of them.

I was told by someone that now I needed to be

filled with the Holy Spirit (they called it Holy *Ghost*). I asked, "How do I get it?"

I was told to go back to the altar and tarry until it comes. So that night I went back. Men beat me on the back while some said to "say this fast, Jesus, Jesus, Jesus." Others said, "That's it, brother, let your tongue go." Some said, "Hold on," while others were saying, "Let go." But after about an hour, one by one they got tired and walked away. This went on for the next three days after I got saved.

On the third night after everyone got tired and I was left alone, tired and weary; I still had my head down in Jesus' sweet lap. As I wept, I said, "Jesus, I don't know why you haven't given me your Holy Spirit. I know I haven't sinned against you since you saved me. But you know what I need." Instantly it was as if someone picked me up off my knees and I was filled with the Holy Spirit and given the gift of tongues.

Now, some may not agree with what I want to say here, but I believe that there are many gifts of the Spirit. There's only one Spirit that we're all baptized into; and everyone who turns to Christ and repents with all their hearts will receive the Holy Spirit, but it isn't tongues that proves it, it's love. "By this shall all men know that you're my disciples if you have love to one another." And besides, no one will have to tell you that you have the Holy Spirit, He'll testify for Himself, and His testimony is true. Just seek God and His righteousness and God will add whatever you need for any reason.

Soon after I got saved, Mildred found out from my uncle that I was going to church and lived in a Christian environment. I had rented a room from a husband and wife who lived right behind the church fellowship hall. She came to church to get back with me. She told me she had only said those things on the phone because Charlie had put her up to it through threats. I told her no, I wouldn't go back to her because now I was a Christian. I was afraid if I did, I would have sex with her and lose out with God. Also, by now I had started sitting beside a girl named Alice who was raised in that church. Alice was a year older than me and someone I thought would be good for me so I'd stay straight. She drove a pretty '56 red Ford Crown Victoria, and when we'd date or double date, she always asked me to drive. Life was looking up again.

CHAPTER 9

I turned 18 and became status 1A with the government draft service. Since the war in Vietnam was going on, I was told that soon I'd be drafted. I went to the army recruiter and joined the Army. I told everyone goodbye and Alice asked me to stay in touch. I boarded a bus for induction center in Charlotte, North Carolina. I and other young men from North Carolina, who had joined, were sent to a hotel in downtown Charlotte to spend the night. We talked about our thoughts about dying for our country. I felt like I was ready to die because of my experience at Alice's church, but I had no intention of dying so people could be proud of me.

I didn't see life like other young men. If I felt pressured or didn't like the way things looked, I had learned from Dad to simply walk away. That feeling of being pressured gripped me from the first day at the induction center where we young men, wearing nothing but underwear, were prodded like cattle into various rooms to be examined from top to bottom. I was poked in every hole of my body. I was terrified and wondered, "What have I gotten myself into?"

I didn't like being controlled and I didn't like the propaganda I heard at the end of the medical examinations. A sergeant came in said, "Men, you're in the Army now. We own you and whatever orders we give you, you will obey. We are the United States' finest fighting machine, so go learn to live to fight or fight to live." Believe me all this talk about learning to fight to live and being owned by the government wasn't what I had expected in the Army.

From day one I was overwhelmed with fear. I had been terrorized as a child with Clifton getting in my face yelling at me, and now every place I went some man in stripes was in my face yelling and threatening me. I was sent on a bus that day to Ft. Jackson, and after not sleeping in Charlotte, then a full day of examinations, and an all-night bus ride, by the time we got to Columbia, I was exhausted. We were herded like cattle.

At Ft. Jackson I was given orders to report back to the bus depot to be sent to Ft. Gordon, Georgia, for basic training. Here I was on another bus going somewhere I'd never heard of and not knowing what to expect.

Once at Ft. Gordon, we were assigned to old barracks that were probably built for World War II or the Korean conflict. They were so uniform that if there weren't names and letters, I couldn't tell which was mine. I was assigned to Charlie Company, 1st Infantry, 1st Battalion. Mildred's dad was named Charlie, and I hated that name. Each time I heard it, it was like he was calling me a hoodlum again. The whole time I was in the Army I never heard anyone talking about Jesus except in cursing, anger, or yelling.

I settled into the Army way of life with reluctance. I didn't want to be there. I had joined and enlisted as a paratrooper because my dad's wife Doris had a son in the paratroopers and that stuck with me. I had no idea what a paratrooper was or what he did. Our first week there consisted of exercises, long marches and learning to stand in formation. Our second week we learned to shine our boots and clean our weapons. By our third week we were soldiers and getting into the best shape we'd ever been. By the fourth week I wasn't even thinking about being a Christian because God wasn't in the Army. I was!

We got our monthly pay on our fourth week and were given the privilege to go to the PX canteen. Everybody went to buy cigarettes, envelopes, writing materials and cosmetics. Then we were allowed to go to the break areas and picnic tables and drink all the (3.2% alcohol) beer we could buy. I soon forgot all about how God had saved me. I slid back into all my old ways.

Our fifth weekend, we were given a 48-hour pass, so my friends and I went to town in Augusta, Georgia. We went from sin-hole to sin-hole, then to a hotel in downtown Augusta to spend the night. Most of us were out of money by now so we went back to our barracks the next day. I went to the chapel service because I felt bad about all the sinning I was doing, but I walked out of there after a brief 30-minute service feeling even worse. The chaplain never mentioned Jesus, His blood, or repentance. All he talked about was being a proud soldier and said, "If you die for your country you'll go straight to Heaven." I just couldn't believe that. I believed if you died in your sins, you'd lose your soul whether a soldier or not.

After eight weeks of basic, we were given a 72-hour

pass and allowed to go home. My orders were to come back to Ft. Gordon Charlie Company for my Advanced Infantry Training (A.I.T.) so I called my mom and asked her could she come to Augusta and pick up me and three friends for the weekend. She agreed and was waiting for us at the off-post pick-up center.

My mom cooked for us and took us to Florence to go to a movie and afterwards, bowling. We had a good weekend and I tried to forget about going back to Ft. Gordon and eight more weeks of what I called Army hell.

I had already qualified as a sharpshooter with the M14, but now I had to be trained in grenades, the self-propelled grenade launcher and any heavier weapon I could master. The night before we had to be back on post for revelry, I went into my mom's bedroom to thank her for being so nice to me and my friends. She was standing gazing out the window. I saw tears running down her face so I hugged her and asked her why she was crying. She said, "I was just praying to the Lord." Up to that point I had never seen my mom pray. She said, "I was praying for you and your friends to come home safe from Vietnam." That startled me because no one on base had mentioned us going to Vietnam. I knew the Bible said not to kill, but the Army was training me to kill people in another country who hadn't done anything to me. I was a confused kid barely 18 years old.

We got back on post and were standing in formation the next day when the sergeant asked, "Is there anyone here who wants to go to truck driving school?" Five or six hands went up. He said, "Step forward and line up to my left." They did.

Then he said, "Is there anyone who wants to be barbers?" Maybe 20 hands went up. He said, "Line up on my right." Once they were out of line, he told the corporal to take the truck drivers to the building that held the lawnmowers and wheelbarrows and divide them up and to divide up the barbers and give them rakes and hedge clippers. I was glad I hadn't volunteered. Then he said, "I need a few more truck drivers so who wants to go to truck driving school? I had loved cutting grass and outside work as a kid so I thought I may as well do it so I raised my hand along with two other soldiers. The sergeant told another corporal, "Take them over to the motor pool for driver's school."

I spent a week learning to drive jeeps and deuce-and-a-half trucks. I would go check out a vehicle each morning, and sometimes I'd drive a captain around in a jeep. Most days I spent driving troops back and forth to various infantry classes. I missed out on a lot of exercises. One day I didn't have to drive and we had a 20-mile walk/run to complete. A few of my friends said, "Windham, you haven't been training with us so you won't make it." I was in tip-top shape even if I hadn't been with them, while one of my friends fell out climbing a steep hill called Misery Hill. When I passed him, the medics had his shirt open pouring water on him. I said, "Hey, Paul, see you at the end."

At the end of our sixth week of A.I.T., a sergeant from the airborne division out of Ft. Benning, Georgia, came to administer the physical test for qualifying to go to jump school. Around 15 or 20 soldiers had enlisted in airborne so we were told we had to run four laps (one mile) around the oval course in less than five minutes, do 10 knee-up crunch sit-ups and five hanging/lift chin-ups. All this was simple for me, my miles carrying a M14 and a 10-pound pack on my back were under the required six minutes.

As I ran, I began thinking about jumping out of an airplane! I was afraid of heights so jumping out of planes wasn't something I wanted to do. After completing the 10 required sit-ups when we got to the simple five pull-ups, I did four and dropped which automatically disqualified me. The sergeant administering the test got in my face yelling, "Soldier, you deliberately did that, get down and give me 50 push-ups" which I did.

My mind was made up that I wasn't going to Vietnam, nor was I going to stay in the Army. I went to the chaplain's office and told him about my convictions against killing someone from another country - someone who hadn't done anything to me. The chaplain had a degree in psychology, so for the next five days he had me come to his office to see if he could get my head straight so I'd take A.I.T. over and make a good soldier. When he finally saw that I wouldn't, he had me discharged from the army as a conscientious objector but under honorable conditions. I was given my mustered-out pay and was on a bus on my way back to North Carolina the next day.

CHAPTER 10

Once in North Carolina, I rented a room at the YMCA in High Point. I had enough money for food for a month and I knew I could find a job by then. On Wednesday, I thumbed a ride to the Church of God for their weekly service. I was standing outside when the people I had grown to love pulled in to park and they all seemed glad to see me. When Alice drove up and parked, she ran to me and hugged me.

We sat together during the service and would write notes back and forth as the service was going on. I told her I would stay at the Y until I could find a job and eventually get closer to her. She told me her aunt had a room available and she'd rent it to me. Then we could drive to High Point to get a refund, gather my things and come back to Thomasville. All of that worked out like she said and for the next month we dated and sat together in church, and got closer.

I got along well with her mom but her dad was cold-hearted and mean-spirited and he seemed to hate the world and everybody in it. He wasn't going to lose his little girl to me. While on a date one night she came up with a plan and suggested we elope and go to my mom's in South Carolina. South Carolina didn't have a three-day waiting period to get married so I went along with it. We left, got our marriage license and got married by the Justice of the Peace the same day. We drove over to Florence to the Holiday Inn to spend the night and consummated our marriage. We drove back to High Point and found an apartment furnished near the hospital and moved in. I soon found a job driving a delivery truck for the High Point Paper Box Company and she went to work as a secretary for a small firm there.

About a week later we decided we had to go face Nelson, her dad. I never heard a man cuss and call me so many names as he did. He blamed me for everything. He was so mean, he told us to leave and leave Alice's car. It was his so he took the keys and we walked away. Alice had everything handed to her all her life so she wasn't used to walking anywhere or thumbing a ride and appreciating the simple things.

Alice and I were going to a house church then and I had rededicated my life to Christ, so I was totally unaware that she wasn't happy until I came home from work to find her gone. Nelson had come and taken her away and left a note saying, "Don't ever come around my daughter again. P.S. I found the pair of women's underwear under the bed." God is my witness if he found a pair of underwear under our bed, he put them there because I loved Alice and I never even thought of another woman, let alone bringing one to our bed. I was only 18 years old and after two months of marriage my world had fallen apart again. I tried in vain for the next two months to talk Alice into coming back home. When I did get to talk to her, she would tell me that she would never come back and hang up, so I finally gave up our apartment and rented a room in the home of one of the brothers and sisters who went to the church I was attending. One night I drove over to Thomasville and parked on a small hill above her house just to see if I could see her. I sat there praying. I remember telling the Lord, "Now what am I going to do? The churches teach that you can only get married once so here I am 18 years old and all I wanted out of life was to love somebody and have children from that love. Now I can't do that."

I drove off but just down the street I saw someone at a red light I thought I knew so I blew my horn and waved. When I drove away a police car got behind me and pulled me over. He said, "There's a law against blowing your horn in town after 9 o'clock so I'm giving you a ticket." Now, remember folks, this is in 1965 and I'm in a small town similar to Mayberry, North Carolina. When he took my driver's license to write me a ticket he said, "Wait a minute. I believe I have a warrant for your arrest for non-support."

I said, "For non-support? How is that possible I don't have a wife anymore and I don't have any children." He said, "I don't know, but I have to arrest you." I had pulled into a parking lot when he pulled me over, so I locked the car doors and he took me to the High Point Jail. I was put in a cell with three other men. One of the men was a nice, respectful man who worked for a plumbing business. He was pulled over in the company truck, and since he didn't have the registration card or proof of insurance, they took him to jail until it got straightened out. I explained why I was in jail and he asked, "Son, you don't look even 15 years old and you're in jail for not supporting a girl you got pregnant?" So, I told him the whole story about me, Alice and her dad.

He told me when I got out, I could come and live at his house, get a job, and pay room and board. Monday morning, I was taken to the family court room before a judge. When I was led in, there stood Nelson, his wife, and Alice. Alice wouldn't even look at me but she was wearing a maternity top and looked very pregnant. Nobody but Nelson and the judge spoke. Nelson started lying to the judge from the start. He told the judge that I made his daughter go with me to South Carolina because I got her pregnant. He told him I drank all the time and ran around on his daughter. So he brought her home and I hadn't even come to check on her. Alice was a virgin when I married her and I never drank or ran around on her. And he failed to tell the judge that I had gone to ask her to come home, but Nelson came out with a pistol and threatened to shoot me if I didn't leave. He lied the first minute his mouth opened.

The judge was prejudiced against me from the start and didn't ask me anything. He just said, "Son I'm gonna make an example out of you today. You'll give this little lady half of your check each week. You'll pay half of her medical bills, and half of her hospital bills and I'm sentencing you to the chain gang for two years, suspended to a year's probation. If you ever come before me again, I'll put you in prison." He rapped his gavel and the probation officer told me to follow him to his office. To this day, I've never seen Alice or her family again and I never saw my daughter until she was 33 years old.

Alice almost made good on her promise when she told me on the phone, you'll never see me or my baby. I left that day for my new friend's home and found a job within a few days as an electrician's helper. The minimum wage back then was $1.25 an hour so for 40 hours a week I brought home $42.00. When I gave the probation officer Alice's half, plus the money for her other bills, I was left with exactly $12.00 and I had to pay $10 a week room and board. I couldn't even buy gas for my car. I did this for two months. Finally, I told my probation officer that I felt stuck in a town that I wasn't from and felt trapped by a woman who was having my baby that she swore I'd never see. I was at my rope's end for an 18-year-old boy. I was in the worst place spiritually and mentally I had ever been. I asked him what would happen if I were to just leave. He said, he'd hunt me down and put me in prison.

I said, "At least in prison I'd get fed, but living like this isn't living. I have no family here and no future."

He said "Don't do it son."

I said, "I'm not. I was only asking."

I believe that if I hadn't said "I'm not, I was just asking," he would've revoked my probation and put me in jail. But my mind was already made up. When I left there, I sold my car to a car lot for $75 and thumbed a ride out of town to the next town of Greensboro so he wouldn't know where I had gone. From there I bought a bus ticket to Long Island, N.Y. where one of Dad's brothers lived in Elmont.

I hadn't made plans with my uncle, but he reluctantly told me I could stay and get a job. I pray that you who are reading this won't judge me too harshly for leaving my responsibilities but wait out the whole story, and before I'm through you'll see how a loving God brought me to Himself a final time. Was it right to leave my child? No. But I have to live with my mistake every day.

I found a job with my uncle's friend who owned a construction company. After work I'd go down to the local pub to drink and try to forget what I had just gone through. I even got a newspaper clipping in the mail from my mom with my little girl's birth date, weight, and length, and I kept it in my wallet for years. She was named Jennifer which was close to Jimmy I thought. My heart was always aching for Jennifer and though I forced myself to not think of her, thoughts of her always tugged at my heart. I tried to push God out of my thoughts because I got bitter against Him. I even told Him once, "How could You let me get tangled up in a church like that? If they're Christians I won't ever be one." I had begun to judge all Christians by Alice. Alice turned out to be just as devious, cold hearted and mean as her daddy.

I didn't care anymore; I got mean and into a lot of fights. I even fought men who I knew had killed before, but I didn't care if I lived or died. My heart was beating in a little baby girl who I thought I'd never get to hold.

One night my cousin Louie and I were riding around drinking whiskey with two girls when they picked up a gang member named Rudy. The drunker we got, the louder and filthier he talked. The girl driving whispered that they'd take him home so we four could be together. Once we got to his house, he started filthy talking to the girls again, so my cousin told him to stop. He jerked the door open and told my cousin to get out. I opened my door, went around to him and told him if he wanted to fight, fight me. He swung at me twice but with one punch I split his face open. Blood poured out of that gash and before he ran off, he said, "I'll kill you, Rebel." Being from the south, I was called Rebel.

We left to park and drink. When we got home the lights were off and glass was on the porch from a busted window pane in the door. The door was locked so we knocked and called. When my uncle Roy came to the door, he said a gang of six young men came looking for me and busted in the door. He told them I wasn't there but before they left, they told him to tell me they would kill me when they saw me. For the next three months, I would be out walking and a car would come to a screeching stop beside me, and guys would pile out with hatchets or hammers and I'd take off running.

One night I came out the back door of the pub and someone yelled, "Run, Rebel. Rudy's got a gun." I fell in the rocks, busted my knee open and tore a big hole in a new pair of pants. I sobered up fast but I had had it. I was never one to run from a fight, so I went to a friend's house because I knew he had a gun. I asked him to loan it to me because I wouldn't run anymore. I was going to kill Rudy. I didn't know it but he knew Rudy. He told me to let him think it over; he was stalling for time. He told Rudy, "The Rebel ain't playing, he's gonna kill you." Rudy asked what should he do? My friend said, "let me get you two together so ya'll can end it." He agreed. Then he came to me and I agreed. We met the next day in front of a gas station and shook hands. I stayed in New York about six months, but I fought and drank the whole time I was there.

I took a bus back to my mom's in South Carolina, but before I left, I called Alice collect. When the operator said you have a collect call from Jimmy Windham, she asked, "Where's it coming from?" The operator told her from Elmont, Long Island, N.Y. I did it to throw her and my probation officer off, because I knew she'd call him and tell him. I was on a bus back to South Carolina the next day.

I was messed up and an angry teenager with a serious chip on my shoulders. I was in tip top shape, a trained fighter and felt like I was running for my life.

If someone just looked at me wrong, I'd do anything I could to provoke a fight and I never lost. I've been shot at, cut, and in so many fights I lost track. At 19, I had already been through more hell than most people go through in a lifetime.

The churches I attended taught that once you married, it was for life, so being young, healthy, and a ladies' man, I made up my mind that I would never set foot in another church. I knew I couldn't live the rest of my life alone. I was mad at the world and at God for taking Jennifer from me. I knew if I had been given just half a chance, I would've made a good husband and the best father to Jennifer.

I remembered Cathy telling me God had His hand on me. I thought, I sure wish He'd take it off because I couldn't take much more. Thank God, He didn't.

CHAPTER 11

When I arrived back in Marion, I called my mom to come get me from the Greyhound bus station. She had moved back to Marion because she had met a nice decent, hard-working man named Shorty Stroud when she was younger and they still liked each other. He was good to my mom and good for her. They lived on Montgomery Street. Carolyn had gotten married, and her husband, Jackie Byrd, had family in Salt Lake City, so they had moved out there. Carolyn was only 13 years old; that in itself shows how our family life had deteriorated. Hal's wife was killed in a car wreck, so Hal lived with my mom who was raising his only daughter.

After I had been there a little while I was told by the unemployment office about a state-sponsored machine shop trade school where I could learn a trade since I was a school dropout, and I would get paid bi-weekly by the State. Hal and I both were assigned to it. The instructor/teacher, Mr. Morris, seemed to like me, and after a week he sold me a car for $20 bi-weekly so Hal and I could get back and forth to school.

Hal had picked up the guitar and told me if I'd get one myself, he'd teach me to play. So, I went to the pawn shop and bought a guitar. He was a natural musician and it seemed that I was too. Before long we were playing and singing country music all around town. I wasn't as devoted to it as Hal, but before long, our music had me forgetting my past.

Next door to Mama's, an elderly woman was raising her teenaged granddaughter. The girl was cute and dark skinned. When I first got there, I asked Hal about her. He said "her name is Bonnie, but hands off because I like her." I learned later that when Hal and I were practicing in our living room, she'd stand outside the window and listen. I had a natural lead voice and Hal sang tenor.

Mama's house was a one-bedroom duplex, so Hal and I slept in the living room on a hide-a-bed sofa. One morning Hal and Mama had gone somewhere. We weren't in school that day and I had slept late. A knock on the door woke me so I opened the door while standing behind it. It was my neighbor, Bonnie. She asked if she could come in. I said "No, I'm in my shorts."

She pushed past me and said, "I've seen a boy in his underwear before." Then she started trying to tickle me in a playful manner. The next thing I knew she was in my arms kissing me. She was young like me, but we both knew what we wanted and we got it. From then on, we'd sneak off together and eventually fell in love. She was exactly what I needed. More on that in a bit.

A man named Slim Mims had a local CBS television program that aired on Tuesday and Thursday mornings. He played country music and was popular in Nashville, and had just been in a movie with Jan-Michael Vincent. He had come back home and invited the local talent to come onto his program.

One day Hal told me that Slim was hosting a talent show in Dillon that night at the high school and he wanted us to audition, so I agreed to go. Whoever won the talent show would be invited to perform on Slim's TV program. The audience picked the winner by clapping. It came down to a young lady, who tapped danced and twirled a baton, and us. The audience clapped the loudest for her, but Slim knew talent so he picked us also and invited us to his show. We became regulars. Back then, we had only one TV station, so everywhere we went, people knew us.

Soon after this I drove over to Florence to see my Daddy. We were hanging out together, drinking whiskey until we both were both pretty well lit. At one point, Daddy told me he loved me and I told him that I'd wade through hell for him. He said, "Really?" I told him I would die for him. He then asked me if I would fight Tommy B.

Allegedly, my mom and Tommy had an affair during one of Daddy's excursions. I asked my dad where Tommy was and he told me he was working as a mechanic at Cox's Motors, So, we headed there. I didn't realize that my daddy and Tommy already had words, and Tommy had told my dad if he came near him, he'd kill him. We parked and walked into the garage area where Tommy worked. I guess even though he was facing his work area, he had seen us come in; because when we walked up and Daddy spoke to him, he turned and swung a ball peen hammer at my dad's head. He missed my dad's head but hit his ear, shattering his ear lobe.

As we jumped back, Tommy yelled, "I told you to stay away from me, Cecil, and I won't tell you again." I

73

asked Tommy what time he got off work and he told me five o'clock calling me, "Boy!" I told him I would see him then. He again called me "Boy" telling me to "go away, Boy!"

Daddy walked away and I followed as he stepped into the office area. He knew Mr. Cox, and he said, "Mr. Cox, look what Tommy B. did to me, and all I did was come in here to get my car fixed."

I looked at my dad's ear with blood was dripping all over his shirt. When I saw that I said, "No way!" I turned around and went back into the garage area. Tommy was still standing there. I grabbed a pull handle from the work area before getting to him. I approached him and saw the hammer that had missed killing my dad by an inch or less still in his hand. Tommy was probably 6 feet, 3 inches and a big man and I was 5 feet 8 inches but I was solid muscle, trained to fight with my fists. As I walked up, I said, "I'll throw mine down if you'll throw yours down."

He said, "Throw it." I tossed it away and he tossed the hammer down.

I was on him so fast. I hit him in the face with a left and as his head and torso went back. I hit him with two quick punches in his stomach. His head and torso came forward and when he fell forward, I grabbed his head between my bicep and right forearm in a death hold and with my left fist I beat him in the face fast and hard about ten times. Each time I'd punch him, I'd say, "Call me 'Boy' now!"

My dad came back in and said, "Jimmy, let him go son, or you'll kill him." I was in a blind rage and probably would have killed him if I hadn't heard my dad. When I let him go, he staggered back toward his work bench. He picked up a wrench and came toward me; but before he got to me, he fell over. My dad and I left, but Mr. Cox heard my dad say that he was going to sue him, so Daddy heard no more from Mr. Cox.

The next day my mama came home and told me that the police were looking for me in Florence because Tommy B. was in a coma in the hospital with both of his jaws wired together. They said if he died, they'd try me for murder.

I left Marion for my uncle's in Lake City. He told me he'd pay me $100 if I'd stay the summer and work on his tobacco farm so I moved in. A week later I called Daddy and told him I was at his brother's in Lake City so he drove over to see me. He told me that Tommy had come out of the coma and was doing fine so no one was going to file any charges. His co-worker told the police that Tommy tried to kill my daddy and I beat him in a fair fight after we both dropped our weapons.

CHAPTER 12

I stayed the summer at my uncle's working in tobacco, and at the end of the summer he paid me. I sold my car, got my guitar, my clothes, and boarded a bus for Salt Lake City, Utah. Hal didn't want me to leave because we had gotten good and were singing in churches around Marion. Mama had moved out to the country where we met a preacher named Brother Padgett. He had a small country church and invited us to sing on Sunday mornings on his radio broadcast. When we left his office to take the platform, there in the audience sat Bonnie next to a man I later found she had married. She was pregnant with her first child. When he came up after the service to shake our hands, it broke my heart to act like I didn't know her but for her sake, I didn't say anything.

But I had to be free and wanted to experience life for myself. It took me three days to arrive in Utah but I enjoyed the trip. One bus driver even had me sit on the step beside him, play my guitar and sing. I ate in the bus station when we had a stop-over to pick up people or change buses and I slept on the bus at night.

Going west was a great experience, and I made up a story that I was going to Utah to college. When someone asked me what I was majoring in, I said, "Music." I was asked also if I was a Mormon, which also sounded nice so I'd say, "Yes," even though I had no idea what a Mormon was or what they believed. One young woman I met on the bus told me she was a Mormon. She saw the cigarettes in my pocket and told me I must be a Jack Mormon, which is to us southerners, like a Baptist. I just agreed with her. When I finally arrived in Salt Lake City, my sister Carolyn and her husband, Jackie, picked me up at the bus station. Jackie now owned a beautiful white '61 Cadillac convertible, and with the top down, he drove me all around Salt Lake City, showing me the sights. Salt Lake City is beautiful, and here I was, a small-town country boy, running from God and the law in a city where I could get lost, but I arrived lost already.

The forefather of Salt Lake City, Brigham Young, came across that mountain and saw the fertile valley, he said, "This is the place;" and when my bus topped that same mountain many years later, I also was astonished by what I saw. I was told that there were seven girls to each guy there, so I decided that day that I'd do all I could to get my seven.

That first week I went out to Kearns because I saw an ad in the newspaper for a machinist job for the Trane Company, building air conditioners. I went there with Carolyn, and because I had my diploma from the trade school I had completed in South Carolina, I was hired making more money to start than most people in South Carolina make after years of work. Jackie's brother, Ray, was a car salesman at a big dealership in Salt Lake City, so Jackie took me there and Ray helped me get a beautiful '58 Pontiac financed. Now things for a 19-year-old boy, who didn't care where life took him, were looking up again.

On the surface, I looked like a carefree young man who had life all figured out. I had a good high-paying job, a sister who loved me, my first precious little niece named Cathy, who I was crazy about, many friends, and a brother-in-law who wanted only the best for me. I always tried to stay out all night, drinking until I couldn't drink anymore, because when the fun stopped and I was alone, everything I had gone through, came crashing in on me. Sometimes I'd even cry myself to sleep because I knew God was near me but I still felt alone and lost.

Utah was a playground for me. Everywhere I went, I could just start talking to a pretty girl and my accent would stop them in their tracks.

Jackie's other brother Rocky owned one of the finest popular night clubs in Salt Lake City where only members or those with reservations went. Girls got in free on Ladies' Night, and there were hundreds of young ladies. He also hired well-known local live country bands. Being family, I got in free with friends. My sister Carolyn and I had learned to dance together as kids so we always took the spotlight when we danced. I would bring my guitar and the bands would ask me to come up and sing a song or two. Again, I was living life to the fullest, and I should've been the happiest 19-year-old alive, but inside I was miserable.

At night, I could still hear Cathy say "God has His hand on you and one day there'll be no place left for you to run." I could still see the look on Bonnie's face when I started to leave. I was leaning against my car and I pulled her to me and kissed her. Then I also remembered the last time I saw her. She was pregnant and she shyly would look at me. I wanted a real life with a wife and kids, and I believed Alice had destroyed all my hopes for that life and had my precious baby girl who I thought of and wondered about every night.

I knew Alice would take care of her, but I also knew nobody could love her like me because she had my heart beating in her little one-year-old chest. I felt like I was being torn in two inside, and only drinking and partying seemed to make it go away. I anchored myself to Bonnie's last words to me when she said, "Jimmy Windham, I've never loved no man but you, and I'll always love you. One day you'll have to let someone love you, because, you may not know it but, you're full of love. One day you'll have to find something or somebody to love." I still got into a lot of fights because even though the girls liked me, guys would get jealous when their girls wanted to talk to me after I sang.

One night I walked outside the club where three men were waiting. The leader said, "Listen country boy, you can dance and you can sing, but can you fight?" He punched me with what I called a sissy punch. I jumped back a little and said, "I grew up fighting before I learned to sing, and if you can't hit no harder than that you're in trouble." I wore all three of them down fast. I had set down my guitar and bottle of beer. The main one pulled a knife from his pocket so I grabbed the beer bottle, broke it on the steps and went towards him. He and his buddies backed away. I never did figure out why they were after me.

Shortly after that I was sitting in the kitchen with my sister Carolyn and Jackie. He was acting strange and kept wanting me to go into the living room with him because he had something to show me. My left hand was in a bandage where I cut my knuckles on one of the teeth of the three men, so I couldn't fight for a while. Finally, I followed Jackie out of the kitchen but just as I reached the living room door, he spun around and punched me in my face. I never expected it or he wouldn't have been able to hit me, but I jumped back and put up my right hand to fight him. He had planned it, because he had a shotgun beside the door so I grabbed a butcher knife off the counter and stood beside the refrigerator next to the door. He said, "Come out." And I said, "No, you come in." We were at a standstill. My sister was in the middle. Finally, he said, "Go to your room, get your things and get out."

My best buddy was Dale Wright, and I left for his house. We had hung out together all the time, and he told me I could always come live at his house when I told him how Jackie was overcharging me. I found out later that Carolyn was always telling Jackie that if he did this or that she'd get me on him. I never had a clue that he was harboring resentment for me over that until he hit me.

I never got over him sucker punching me, but I finally got even with him. I went to visit them after we were supposedly past that ordeal, and this time as we sat in his kitchen drinking, he said the wrong thing to me, but he was hemmed in.

I stood up and said, "You can't get to your gun this time, Jackie, and I owe you a beating." He tried to get around me but I picked him up in one arm, opened his door with my left hand and took him outside to whip him.

It wasn't funny then, but it is now because he latched down on my thumb with his teeth and I no longer wanted to fight. I wanted him to let go. I said, "I give, Jackie, I give!"

He mumbled, "If I let go do you promise to go back inside and drink another beer with me?"

I said, "I promise." He let me go and we went back inside.

He said, "Now we're even. But I knew one day you'd want revenge on me." What he didn't know was I used to lay in bed and think of how I would finally get even with him. I planned to really beat him down when I did get him alone, but I learned that night that he wasn't a fighter; to me he was a cheater. He hid behind his guns and it's alleged that eventually he killed a young man who he thought was his son because his son and him had fought. His son gave his ball cap to his buddy, and when he came out of the bar someone shot him in the head. It wasn't proven, but anyone who knew Jackie knew that he was capable of it.

I know this much, I never trusted him. My sister married him when she was 13 years old and had his three children. Once he became a rich man from his car garages around Salt Lake City, he kicked Carolyn to the curb and married a younger woman.

I moved into Dale's daddy's home. His dad loved Eddie Arnold, who was called the "singing cowboy," and I'd go in the living room and sit with him as he played Eddie's songs over and over. He drank crème de cola liqueur and I'd drink blackberry brandy. I grew to love him like the father I felt I never had. He wouldn't take money from me for living there even when I tried to pay him.

I could talk to him about my loneliness and empty feelings, and I would listen as he told me his. I found out his ran a lot deeper than mine, because he drove his car to a beautiful place up the mountain above Salt Lake City called Lookout Point and committed suicide. I've driven up there many times with dates and drank beer and looked out over the city. In that same beautiful spot, he ran a hose from his tailpipe into his window and fell asleep in death. That hurt me so bad and scared me until I left Utah.

CHAPTER 13

My life was about to take another startling change. From living in Florida with my dad at 16 until now was just over three short years. I was barely 20 years old and had already been through enough to last a lifetime. I felt that every time I loved someone, I'd lose them, so I was afraid to let myself love anyone. Dale's dad taking his life scared me because it seemed that it was so easy for him to do that, and I was afraid that one day it would be easy for me.

When I was alone at night in bed, I battled thoughts of ending my life with a hose pipe running into my car window. The only thing that kept me from doing that was, while Dale's dad never knew God because he was a Mormon, I had felt God's Spirit in me.

I had been taught suicide was wrong and truthfully, I was afraid to meet God. I lived like He didn't exist. I was rebellious! I didn't want God controlling my life because I knew all the things I was enjoying was against His Word. I was sleeping with every girl I met, drinking, smoking, and staying out all night. I was free from restraints and no one was ever going to tell me what to do again.

In the deepest part of my soul I wanted to be controlled and to be able to come home from work and look into the eyes of my little girl, Jennifer. But I knew because I left, I would never be able to do that, and the guilt was killing me. Some men are deadbeat dads by choice, while I felt I was forced to be one due to situations that were overwhelming to an 18-year-old boy.

I was now over 20 years old, yet still not a man. I was living like a teenager while men my age were starting families and careers. I had no direction, no leadership, and no foundation except for the year I spent in the boys' home. I lived for fun and from one paycheck to the next. I never saved a dime. I went to work on Monday morning broke and worked all week to get paid. Some Monday mornings I woke up in my car in the parking lot where I worked and drank a stale beer before walking inside to start all over again. My life was going nowhere fast. But as I said, I left Utah after Dale's dad committed suicide.

I had become friends with a young man who had parents in Salt Lake City but he lived on the streets, sponging off friends or whatever he could hustle or steal. Lots of nights we'd party down on the strip on 2nd South St. where the night life, hookers, and drugs were. I shot up heroin my first and only time there one night with a hooker I had met named Bee Bee. She called me "home boy" because she was from North Carolina and I was from South Carolina. She already had the money she needed for her fix and had bought her smack. She took me to her room, had sex with me and then she shot me up with heroin. I was in a dark dirty bathroom over a flashing neon beer sign with a needle in my arm. I began to throw up so she left me. I was alone and, as God is my witness, I felt like I was dying, so I cried out, "Please God, don't let me die like this." Instantly the room lit up and not because of a light switch. As I walked out of there, Bee Bee looked surprised and said, "Aren't you high?"

I said, "No, I feel fine" and left.

Dale had a married sister who lived in a suburb of Minneapolis who came to visit. I drove her all over Salt Lake City. Since I was young and carefree, Dale's sister asked if I'd drive her back to Minnesota; she didn't like to fly. I could stay at her house with her, her husband and two boys and get a job. After a few nights with her, and she showing me what else I'd be getting, I agreed to drive her back to Minnesota. She cashed in her plane ticket and we took off.

I remember crossing Wyoming, part of Nebraska, and South Dakota. I made a wrong turn in South Dakota and entered North Dakota, so I tried taking small roads back into South Dakota. At one point the weather was bad and the skies were as dark as night, and even with my gas pedal to the floor, the car would only go about 50 miles an hour. She kept screaming at me to get off the road. The tail end of my car would swing around at times, but I was scared so I just kept going. When we got to the next town it was night time and I pulled into a gas station.

The attendant asked me which way I had come from and when I told him he said, "You're a lucky man because a tornado went down that road and tore everything up in its path." I had outrun a tornado. Tornadoes in the South were almost unheard of, so I asked her about tornadoes. Once she told me, I realized I was afraid of nature's violence. I knew God controlled nature and I was afraid of God. She told me that tornadoes were very common in Minnesota because of all the lakes there. I thought, I won't be staying long.

We arrived at her house after two days and nights on the road. She introduced me to her husband and a few friends who were waiting on us to get back from Utah. I liked her husband from the start, so I decided fast that I would change my direction with her. He wasn't anything like she had described. They had a nice home with a basement that they used for parties. I was given a bedroom in the basement, and made comfortable. That weekend they held a party to welcome her back. They had so many friends that the whole house was crowded with people, and everywhere I turned someone was asking me to have a drink with them. I was glad that my bedroom was close because, after a long trip and all that whiskey, I got too drunk to party and went to bed.

Sometime later I felt my bed shaking and I turned to find her getting into bed with me. I jumped out of that bed fast. She asked what was wrong, so I told her that I wouldn't be her boy toy anymore. When she asked me why, I told her that when we were in another state that was one thing, but now that I'd met her husband and liked him, I couldn't do this anymore. She cussed a little and left.

I began to see him differently also. A little later in the week her husband asked me one evening if I'd help him get out of the house by saying I wanted to go play pool with him. I asked him and he said, "Sure, we'll go do that." He kissed her and we left. I still didn't know what he had in mind when he pulled down a dirt road. But right behind us another car pulled in with a pretty young thing driving. She came to his van and I recognized her from the party. She got in the back and he asked me would I mind going and sitting in her car. I did and, as I sat there, I thought about him and his wife cheating on each other so I didn't feel quite as bad for sleeping with her a few times, but I also told myself that I needed to get out of there as soon as I could.

I saw an ad in the paper for a machinist at the Federal Cartridge Corporation so I applied. I was given a job and they paid twice as much per hour more than the other company around. They made bullets for the U.S. Government to be used in the Vietnam War. It was a large company with buildings sitting on a square mile of land. They had machines that cut a groove in the brass jacket of the bullet. It also had a division that packed cartridges with gunpowder and lead, but that was a high-paid section, and it took years to transfer to one of those jobs.

I was assigned to the scrap brass sector. The scrap brass that is cut out of the grooves of the cartridges is saved and collected in barrels. Someone would place the barrels of shavings on the back dock and I would go around all day collecting the barrels and carry them to our plant where we unloaded them. We had a bailing machine and a *bailer* would make bales of the shavings. Then we'd load up the bails with a forklift and take them to another plant where they would be melted down and the process of making shells would start all over. I liked the man who was our driver because he was originally from Texas so he talked like me.

After about a week of working with him and others on our truck, I told him about the man and woman who took me in. He told me he had an extra bedroom at his house and, if I wanted, I could come live there. He set a weekly price that I'd pay for room and board and I'd ride to work with him. When I got my first check, I gave some money to the husband where I was living, told them goodbye and moved in with Gary. He was a good cook so I ate good, but he was also an alcoholic and drank mixed drinks every night.

I went out a lot, so I began to meet girls that I would bring home. Then God moved for me to meet a young lady. I said God led me, and soon I'll tell you why I said it was God. I went to Target one day almost drunk and though I had money in my pocket, for some strange reason I picked a coat off the rack and slung it across my shoulders, paid for my other purchases and proceeded to walk out of the store with the coat still over my shoulders. At the door I was approached by the store's security agent, who asked me to follow him upstairs. I was arrested for shoplifting but allowed to post my own bond without going to jail.

At that very instant across town at another store a young woman put some eye mascara, eye liner, and a few little things in her purse and was also arrested for shoplifting and, like me, was also able to post her own bond.

Gary fussed at me for doing something so dumb and childish but it was done and the next week I had to go to court for the shoplifting charges. Gary told me not to worry over it because it was a misdemeanor and all I'd have to do was pay a fine. Across town the young woman was assigned the same court date and, like me, she also had a good job. She worked at Ben Franklin Company as a computer key punch operator.

The morning I went to court people were milling around in the hallways or in a room adjoining the courtroom where there were snacks, coffee, and soda machines. I noticed two ladies who came in and got coffee. The older one sat down, but the younger one was pacing the floor and nervous. I already knew what to expect because Gary had told me, so I had taken money out of the bank to pay my fine. I started a conversation with the older one. I finally asked her if she'd like to go out with me sometime. She said she would but she was already in a relationship so she couldn't. But she said, "My friend just moved to Minneapolis from Albert Lea and doesn't know anyone yet" (God also led her!). She said that her friend whose name is Susan was nervous because she had to see the judge for shoplifting.

I went over to Susan and told her, "Look, I know you're nervous, but you'll be all right and all you'll have to do is pay a fine. When this is over, will you let me take you and your friend out to lunch?"

She was still very nervous and said, "I don't know, we'll see."

My case was called right after that. The judge was condescending as he told me I had a good job, a nice home, etc., and had no reason to shoplift and fined me $25. When I came out to where Sue and her friend was, I told her what I had done and what the judge had said to me and about my fine so I noticed she relaxed a little. Our lives were perfectly parallel. Two months earlier we both had left home to come to Minneapolis. A week earlier on the same day at approximately the same time of the day we were put on a collision course with each other and our destiny. Three months later she'd be pregnant with my beautiful baby girl, Shelley, and a month later we'd be married. I said it was all led by God and you'll agree as we go along. She too went before the judge and was fined $25.

They started to leave without saying goodbye, but Sue's friend handed me a piece of paper with Sue's name and phone number. I called a few nights later and we talked for hours. She invited me to supper the next night, but when I rolled up in front of their apartment, she came out and asked if it would be okay if we went out instead. From that point on we were together every night. Gary's girlfriend owned her own home and sometimes he'd be gone from Friday evening until Sunday, so Sue and I spent those weekends together.

One night while lying on the living room floor and listening to music, she told me she was pregnant. I told her, "We'll get married and I'll raise that baby, but I've got some things to tell you first." I told her everything that happened to me in North Carolina and that I had a daughter named Jennifer that I couldn't see. Then I said, "If you marry me, I want you to know that I may never settle down anywhere. And I believe that one day I'll have to give myself totally over to God to do a work for Him. Also, I've been taught that if I marry you, I will be living in sin, so I don't know what I'll do. But, let's take it a day at a time and raise our baby together."

She agreed, so we got married on Jan. 25, 1969, in St. Paul, Minnesota, with her mom and dad present. Soon after that, we moved to an apartment in Albert Lea where I got a job. My precious little girl Michelle Marie (Shelley) was born on Sept. 29, 1969, exactly four years and 19 days after Jennifer was born.

Sue was a perfect mother and wife. I did not deserve such a good wife, but God, in all His mercy and love, gave her to me to help me survive. I was unfaithful to her many times in our marriage, but she never left me or even complained. She had to be an angel from heaven sent to earth with a mission of helping me find my way. When we stand before God, I know He'll give her a crown, because every gray hair on her precious head I put there because I was so lost. She endured 14 years of my antics and hell and, believe me, she deserved so much better than me. All I can say is, "God bless that dear woman wherever she is."

I was 22 when Shelley was born and soon, my drinking and partying were too much for Sue's parents, and I came home one night to find Sue and Shelley gone. The next day I drove over to their home to find out what was going on. I rang the doorbell, but no one would come to the door so I left and went to the phone and called their home. Sue's mom Phyllis answered. I asked her where my wife and baby were. She said, "*If* you ever want to see Sue and Shelley again you've got a lot of changing to do first."

I was living North Carolina's torture all over again. But I made up my mind that this time I would be smarter and I *wasn't* going to leave without my baby. For the next two weeks, I called and politely asked Phyllis if I could I talk to Sue. I'd bring Sue flowers and sit in the living room and talk. Phyllis was holding Shelley hostage and wouldn't let me see her, but I had a plan and I was sticking to it. Finally, she let Sue go out with me and, and later one evening she let Shelley go with us. I drove to our house and we went in. Most of Shelley's stuff was still in our bedroom, so I started packing mine and Shelley's stuff. Sue asked me what I was doing, so I told her that I and Shelley were leaving for Utah and if she wanted to come, she needed to pack. She immediately packed. She said she was so tired of her mom complaining all the time and was glad I came for them. I told her now Phyllis will experience what I felt when she took my daughter and I would try to never let her see Shelley again. It was 13 years before she'd see Sue or Shelley again.

We left that night for Utah. When we arrived in Utah I drove to my sister's home because that's where I always went, but Jackie must've been tired of me just dropping in, because the day we got there he took me outside and told me, "You can stay here until you find a job but when you get your first check I want you to find another place to stay."

Sue and I both had worked in a furniture factory so we both got hired at Carla's Kitchen Cabinets not far from Jackie's home. When we got off work, we had to ask our supervisor for a loan so we could get something to eat, because Jackie and Carolyn were giving us the cold shoulder. I told Sue it was because they wanted us to leave. But Jackie had already made his feelings known to me from day one. I went to our supervisor and told him that we couldn't stay and asked him to pay us up to 12 o'clock Friday afternoon so we would have all our income. He told us he hated to lose us, but we'd have all our income for all our hours Friday afternoon.

When we got paid and went back to Jackie and Carolyn's home. I told Carolyn we were leaving town for good. She wanted us to stay and rent a place close to them, but I pointed out how they had made us feel unwelcome by shunning us and how Jackie had told me from day one we weren't welcome. She told me Jackie had put her up to the cold shoulder routine so we would want to move but not out of town, just to an apartment. I tried to give her some money for staying there but she wouldn't take it so we hugged and cried and left.

I had no idea where I was going. I was such an impulsive person that when we finally crossed the mountain leading out of Salt Lake City into Wyoming I came to a divide in the freeway. One way led to Casper, Wyoming, and the other way led to Denver, Colorado. I pulled into the middle of the split and I looked up and told God, "I've been run off again and made to feel like I'm not wanted by my own family and here I sit in the middle of the freeway, one going left and one going right. I don't know where to go so the next car that comes along is the one I'll follow." The next car that came went toward Denver, so I started my car and headed towards Denver.

CHAPTER 14

When we arrived on the outskirts of Denver it was very late, so I pulled into a gas station to get coffee and a newspaper. I found an ad for a furnished apartment downtown so I parked beside the station and we slept until morning. Once the sun came up, I awoke and went to a pay phone to call the manager at the apartment house. A man answered and told me the apartment was still available. I told him I'd be there shortly to rent it. I didn't have much money above the price of the apartment. I knew I needed the apartment though and I'd have to find work fast to feed my wife and baby girl. The service station attendant directed me downtown and to the street with the apartment.

I found the apartment in a rundown area of downtown. It was in a wooden building with two one-bedroom apartments upstairs over two downstairs. And next door was a building with about 10 rooms to rent. I saw a few men who looked like winos walking into that building, so I was wondering, what am I doing here? The man who owned the building took me upstairs to show us the apartment, he used the kitchen table to put out the cigar he was smoking. The table fell over because it only had three legs. We entered through the kitchen which had a bathroom off to its right and a straight shot into the adjoining bedroom with a straight shot into the living room. It only had three rooms. All the furniture was old and tattered but I rented it.

When he left, Sue asked, "What are we going to do?"

All I could say was "I don't know." I had never felt as insecure as I did at that moment. I walked into the bedroom and got on my knees, and I prayed asking God to help me. We made it through the night on an old saggy mattress with no sheets. The next morning, I went downstairs to the manager's apartment to ask directions to a store that sold sheets and pillows. He was a friendly old man who had two kids and a very talkative wife. She volunteered to give us some sheets, pillows and a few odds and ends of pots and pans so I accepted.

The old man and I sat down and talked. I told him about leaving Salt Lake City and that I needed a job. He said, "Let's get you comfortable and then I'll help you find a job." He told me where a local supermarket was so I drove there and bought some food, diapers, baby food and milk for Shelley to last about two weeks plus a case of beer. When I returned Sue had cleaned and swept and cooked breakfast.

Afterwards I went down to the old man's apartment to look in the paper for a job. I saw a few prospects that I circled, and Pops said I could come to where he worked on Monday and use the pay phone. He worked at the Salvation Army Thrift Store about three blocks from where we lived. He, along with two men assigned to his truck, would drive to homes where people were donating furniture and clothing to the Salvation Army. This was the main store, so they had five or six trucks on the road at all times with a large intake store attached behind the main store. Men, who were winos or just down on their luck, worked there sorting out clothes and furniture that was priced by an employee and sent out to the stores around Denver. I went to the manager's office and told him a little about myself and asked for a job. I was hired right then working on the back dock unloading trucks at minimum wage.

A few days after I had been working on the dock, I was on break, so I walked into the back door of the store. I browsed around for a while just looking and watching the ladies who worked as they sold items people needed. A woman came up to me and asked if I worked there. I said, "Yes, I work out back."

She said, "Come here," and took me to a refrigerator that had a tag for $50. She said, "I can't afford but $40. Will you take it?"

I thought to myself, "This stuff is free and $40 is better today than $50 who knew when." So, I pulled the $50 tag off and said, "I'll be right back." I went to one of the sales ladies and asked could I borrow her sales book. She looked at me strangely but didn't know who I was so she handed it to me. I asked her, "What's your name?" She told me so I wrote her down as the sales person and sold that lady that refrigerator for $35 and winked when I put $5 in my pocket. I went back to work on the dock, but in a short while I was paged to the manager's office. I thought, "Oh, boy, I'm in trouble because he found out about my pocketing the $5." When I walked into his office, he had a stern look on his face and said, "Who told you that you could go into the main store?"

I said, "Nobody. I was on my break."

He said, "Who told you to sell a refrigerator to a woman customer?"

I said, "Nobody, she asked me to help her."

He said, "Do you like selling things?"

I knew I wasn't in trouble by now. I said, "Yes sir, I do, sir."

He said, "I'm writing you out a voucher for $25 so you can go in the store and buy nice dress clothes, because starting tomorrow morning you'll be a salesman in the main store."

Listen, don't ever pray in desperation if you don't expect God to move for you. I may not have been a Christian when I prayed outside Casper, Wyoming, for God to lead and help me, or when I prayed beside that rundown bed, but I know that God helps the needy if they're sincerely desperate. That $5 I pocketed was a lot in 1970, and the $25 bought me a wardrobe. I bought a crib for Shelley with the $5 that was priced $15. That whole week I sold so much stuff for the store and I made a lot for me and my family. It seemed I could sell anything.

I became friends with all the truck drivers and would tell them what furniture I needed and when I'd get home each day, I found beautiful, used furniture delivered to and set up by these men. In return, I'd buy a carton of cigarettes for each one on that particular truck. Soon I had a beautifully furnished apartment with everything we needed. When pretty baby clothes came in on a truck the workers would set them aside for Shelley.

The man who owned the building came to my apartment one evening as he would do from time to time and he always loved to hold Shelley. Under my watchful eye I'd let him, but Shelley was a serious Daddy's girl. If I wasn't at work, I was home and from the minute I got home Shelley was in my arms or on my lap. She would be in her crib when I came in from work and she'd hear me open the door. That crib would get a beating as she tried to get out of it to get to me. I'd peek around the corner, because she was looking for me, then I'd jump back. She'd start jerking that crib again saying, "DaDa." I wouldn't let her wait long. I'd rush in and pick her up. Anyways, the owner was there visiting us, holding Shelley. The man owned a lot of property around Denver and was wealthy. He was serious when he said to me, "Jimmy, I'll write you a check for half a million dollars if you'll let me adopt Shelley."

I looked at him in silence for a minute as he waited for my answer. I said, "If you'll add another half million to your check, you can watch me tear it up because I wouldn't sell you my baby for all of your money. I lost one of my babies and I'd give a million if I had it to get her back, so keep your money."

One thing I can say truthfully is I may not have been a good husband because my religion told me I wasn't really married in God's eyes, so I cheated often and drank every day and night. But anybody who knew me could tell you that I loved and respected my children more than anything or anybody alive. If you wanted hell with a capital H on your hands, just mess with one of my kids. I didn't care who you were, I would come to get you.

An example of how I cared for and protected my children is after my youngest son, David was born (recorded later in this book), he came running into the house crying as I sat in my recliner and said, "Daddy, Daddy, the principal whipped me."

I sat up and said, "Why son? What did you do?"

He said, "I didn't do anything. Some boys behind my desk were talking and cutting up so the teacher sent us to the principal's office and he whipped us."

I said, "Did you tell him you weren't talking?"

He said, "Daddy, I tried but he wouldn't listen to me."

Bear in mind that if David were guilty of anything, he surely wouldn't be telling me, he'd be trying to hide it. I put him in my truck and I couldn't get to that school fast enough. We walked down that hallway into an area with two desks separated by a long wooden bar with two offices behind it all. One had a name tag with "Principal" on it. Two ladies were working at one of the desks. I said very loud, "Is the principal here?" They didn't know what to say, but he heard me and walked out of his office and said, "I'm Mr. So and So, I'm the principal. What can I do for you?"

I said, "Mr. So and So, I didn't raise a liar and my boy told you he wasn't talking in class and you whipped him anyway. If you ever put your hand on my son again, I'll beat your (blank) out there in the yard in front of all these little children. Do you understand me?"

He was as white with fear. He said, "Uh, I'm-m-m sorry, David."

I looked down at my son and said, "Is that good enough for you, David?"

David said, "Yes, sir, Daddy." So, I took my son's hand and led him away. All I'm saying is I know I was a dog when it came to being a husband, but I would die for any of my children, and the one who was taken from me didn't know how much I loved her and missed her until she finally got to know me years later. More on that later.

When I arrived in Denver six months earlier, I was very poor and needy. Now I was assistant manager at the main store; and besides making a good salary, I was making money on the side by giving everyone discounts and a tip for me. Sue, Shelley and I dressed in nice expensive clothes that rich people donated to help the poor and the needy.

I stayed in Denver for about a year. Sue got pregnant again but had a miscarriage. Just prior to her miscarriage I got drunk in our back yard with the old man and a Mexican. The Chicano kept disrespecting me in front of my wife and the old man and his family, so I warned him. He was a big man who was used to shoving his weight around, so my warning only made him laugh. Before He could retaliate, I had his head going backwards from hard fast punches in his face. He was a bleeder and his blood poured. He slept in one of the rooms next door, and as he was trying to get in his room, I was shooting down the hallway at him with my .22 rifle. He moved out the next day. He told the manager that I was a crazy man and he was afraid that I'd kill him.

Anyway, Sue had a miscarriage, and in Denver when a woman had a miscarriage, a psychologist was called in to treat her for depression. When she told him just a little about me, he came and took Sue and Shelley to a halfway house to get them away from me. He told me that unless I agreed to see a marriage counselor and a psychiatrist, he would give Sue and Shelley a bus ticket to anywhere she wanted to go. My fears of losing my baby came back, so I told him I'd do anything. I cleaned out the refrigerator and stopped drinking and I prayed hard for God to not let me lose my wife and little girl. I got desperate again.

The next day Sue came over under supervision to get her and Shelley's things and I told her I had stopped drinking and smoking. I told her if she'd give me another chance I'd change. She still packed and told me she had a bus to catch back to Albert Lea to her mom's and it was already set up. I hugged her bye and cried as she left. I went inside and fell on my knees and I begged God to please not let me lose my little girl. I promised Him if He'd send them back, I'd serve Him. I must've cried for an hour. I heard the back door open and Sue say, "Jimmy." I ran to the kitchen and she stood there with Shelley in her arms and suitcases beside her. Shelley held her little arms out and I took her. Sue said, "That psychiatrist said it's your past causing you to do what you do. But he saw how much you love Shelley and how much she loves and needs you, so we agreed you deserve another chance."

Shortly after that, Sue and I started going to church. We told the people about our past lives, and again I was told that because I had been married to Alice for three months, Sue wasn't my real wife and we were living in adultery. So, I told Sue to sleep in one bedroom and I'd sleep in another, so I could raise my daughter. One night one of those church biddies was straightening me out with her doctrine and asked me if I was still sleeping with Sue. I was trying to live for God so I wouldn't lie, so I said, "I went to her bed once since rededicating myself."

She said, "She's not your wife."

I don't know why, but I said, "God, if she is my wife let her become pregnant."

That biddy said, "Well I'll agree with that. But you have a daughter, so if God gave Sue to you, let her be pregnant and let it be a son."

CHAPTER 15

We left Denver shortly after that for South Carolina and in the Florence Memorial Hospital, nine months later, I tiptoed into Sue's bedroom where she had my first precious son, Jimmy Jr., who's left handed like me, and as God is my witness, in the center of his little back was a drop of blood with a cross in it. That went away in about two weeks. God had once again heard my desperate cry and answered me from Heaven. We came from Denver back to Florence and moved in with my dad who had married a girl less than half his age and she had my dad's child about the same time my wife Sue had our son.

I went to work for the Federal Housing Authority in Florence. I was given a company truck and a two-bedroom apartment in the center of the Projects that included a telephone, and heating and cooking gas. My dad and his new family lived in the apartment next to mine. Dad and I drank together again because now I had stopped going to church. I was 27 years old now, but the loneliness and insecurities had never left. On the surface, I appeared happy, well-liked and friendly. But my soul was troubled. I felt lost from God and scared all the time. I always felt depressed and alone, I was confused and disturbed. I didn't like crowds and I had no male friends. I had to buy over-the counter sleep aids or drink myself to sleep.

After another miscarriage, Sue had another son that I named William Keith and called him Billy.

Every morning I went to work at various apartments where tenants had moved out, leaving a mess, broken windows or holes in the Sheetrock. As the lead, I'd have my crew do repairs so the unit could be rented again. On weekends, I was on call, so I was always busy. I also had taken up fishing in the evenings and weekends, so that kept me busy. Shelley had her own special place in my life, but now I had two little boys who had become my life. I taught them how to fix things. Jimmy always wanted to know the how and why, but Billy wanted to take things apart to see what made them work. I loved being a dad, and I had the best kids alive. But the emptiness never seemed to go away, and I always felt like it was me against the world. It seemed like a waste of time trying to acquire things. After two years, I began to have severe bouts of depression, and I was tired of living in the same house, going to work every day doing the same thing.

I had met a preacher in Denver who had a radio ministry with a large following; he was warning people to get out of the big cities, move to an area he said God designated as a "blessed area" and grow and store up food for a famine that was coming.

The preacher sent out a newsletter every month or so; and he had scheduled a two-week revival in Dothan, Alabama, so I determined that I would be at that meeting. My soul was crying out for change and I had to do something. It was my way to keep moving, I had been too long in one place already. I had learned from my dad when I tired of coping with life, just pack up and leave. I told my supervisor at work, then told my dad I was leaving.

Everybody, especially my dad, argued and begged me to not leave. But when I got my check, I sold or gave away the things I had acquired and left for Nashville because I wanted my brother Hal to go to Dothan with me.

Hal had moved to Nashville, to try to break into music, but he had been there for two years and hadn't made it big. I was told that he was singing back-up for groups and singles who were also trying to make it. With that being said, I knew he probably wouldn't ever be a lead singer.

When we got to Nashville it was in the middle of the day so I drove to where Hal worked. He took us inside and showed us around the studio. He introduced us to his friends and then introduced me to the owner. Hal began telling him how we had sung on TV and in churches back home, so he asked us if we'd sing for him. I really didn't want to but Hal kept insisting so I finally agreed. I hadn't had time to tell him why I was there or where I was going. I was only there to try to persuade him to go to Alabama to the tent revival. But I went to the car and came back with my guitar, and Hal and I sang the country song we loved best called *Don't Be Angry*.

Now before God, I'm telling you exactly what happened. Hal's boss picked up the phone when we stopped singing and called someone. He said, "Listen, you told me you were looking for a "brother" talent. Well, I've just listened to two boys who sing and look like the Everly Brothers here so I'll bring them over to see you."

When he hung up, he asked us to put our guitars in his car and he drove us across town to another recording studio. I don't remember the name but it was a major label and not small like the one Hal worked for. We were ushered into the owner's office and asked to sing so we took out our guitars and sang *Don't Be Angry*. When we stopped that man said, "Boys, I've looked for you for a while now, so be here tomorrow morning because I'm going to make you famous."

We left and all night I told Hal that I wasn't staying, and he'd counter with, "But, Jimmy, this is what we've waited on all our lives." He argued that he'd tried to break into music for two years and we sang one song as a duo and the world was being offered to us.

I argued that this was his dream not mine. I just knew that along with Nashville and fame and fortune came Satan, drugs, drinking, women, and more misery than I already had, so I wasn't staying.

We argued back and forth all night. The next morning as I was putting my stuff back in my car and as Hal stood at the trunk of my car he said, "You're really not going to stay, are you?"

I said, "No, I only came to get you, Hal."

He said, "Then give me a moment to pack my suitcase." We left for Alabama.

When we arrived at the site, there were tents and campers of all sizes everywhere on the grounds. I had bought a tent because we had already been to some of these meetings and I knew what to expect. Once our tent was up, I drove to Dothan and bought food for quick meals. I bought ice for our cooler and milk for Billy who was a baby at that time. I bought propane gas for our cook stove and I stopped by a car lot and asked the manager if he needed a mechanic. I told him I was with the gospel tent crowd that came to be revived. He gave me a job tuning up used cars, so I would go to work each morning and then go hear Bro. T. preach at night. I estimate that each service had over 1,000 people under the tent. On the first night's service, Bro. T. felt led to walk down the aisles and minister by word of knowledge. He came to the row where we were sitting in and asked Hal to come to the aisle and asked him to raise his hands. He looked at Hal and said, "It's not by accident that you're here tonight. God called you to sing and preach the gospel for Him." He laid his hand on Hal and instantly Hal was filled with the Holy Spirit, and until Hal went to sleep in Christ, he never sang country music again. He made gospel tapes of the songs he wrote and he preached wherever he found an open door. So, I know God sent me to Nashville to get him and take him to Dothan, Alabama.

Bro. T. had a local congregation at Dothan so we started going to the church there. I changed jobs and found an apartment for us to live in. I went to work operating heavy equipment for a small landscaping company there in Dothan, so I was making a decent wage.

The church we attended had a lot of division in it and the pastor was caught taking money, so we didn't stay long in Alabama. I had heard that Bro. T. had opened a "blessed area" in South Carolina, so we left for upstate South Carolina near Georgia. I found a house out in the country near Walhalla or West Union and we went to church in Westminster. This church had a pastor who split with Bro. T. over money so I was cautious. I noticed everyone who attended his church would give until they had nothing left to give and end up unable to pay their bills, and these preachers who lived in nice brick homes and drove new cars would still beg for more money. I was trying to find God in my life but though I was skeptical of these churches, I felt I had nowhere else to go.

I've always been good in the construction trade so I started subcontracting work for roofing companies and painters. Before long I had hired three brothers from the church and was making a lot of money tearing off old roofs, re-decking and re-shingling them. By now my last boy was born, and I named him David T. in honor of the pastor of the church we attended. I was doing so good in my business and my crew and I had work all over Tiger Paw where we lived near Clemson, so I decided to expand over into Georgia. The town of Toccoa was on the same main road that ran from Greenville to Marietta, so I moved over into Toccoa into a four-bedroom house.

Now I had a nice home, four wonderful children, cars, trucks, motorcycles and money in my pocket. I still attended Bro. T.'s church in Westminster because, though some of his pastors weren't right with God, I believed I still knew Bro. T. to be a fasting, praying man, and I had hopes that he'd straighten things out eventually. I'd work, spend time with my family, and we'd attend the Sabbath service each Saturday morning and evening.

The only thing in life that seemed to give me peace and joy was raising my four children. I loved them so much and I tried hard to never let them go through what I went through as a child. I showed my love for them in every way, but I also had a firm hand to discipline them if they needed correcting.

I didn't drink the 14 years I was blessed to spend with my children, but I still had an eye for a hot little pretty girl and on occasion I would still cheat on Sue. Sue knew what was going on but because she wouldn't say anything, I felt she didn't really love me, so I stopped caring. Sue never showed any affection and I felt we were only living together to raise the kids. I'm not blaming her because if I had a wife who ran around on me, I wouldn't want to touch her either, I blame myself for how Sue treated me. It wasn't until I came to prison and had to finally face my past, that I saw what a dog I was to such a good woman. I put the gray in her hair and the wrinkles on her face and if I could go back, knowing what I know now, I would've loved her perfectly and protected my home and served God with all my heart. I was still on the run from my childhood, and I didn't know how to live a normal life. Thank God for the blood of Jesus.

Any normalcy I possessed I learned on my own. I loved my kids and tried to give them a strong foundation. I think I held on to sanity and strength because I loved them so much and I anchored to them. I needed them more than they needed me. I was beginning to feel myself slipping away.

CHAPTER 16

I needed change and fast, because I was again feeling emptiness and loneliness. The change came after one of Bro. T.'s preachers, Bro. Dave, from San Antonio, came to hold a revival in our church. He was a very likable fiery preacher who had the appearance of a distinguished older gentleman. The first night of the revival, he was taking up an offering, I slipped a hundred-dollar bill into his hands after the service. Since he was staying in a motel in Toccoa where I lived and was very likeable, I told him to meet me for breakfast at the Huddle House. I didn't know it then, but he was very devious, out for himself only, and playing on my sincerity from the moment I put that money in his hand. As I'd soon find out, he was a wolf in sheep's clothing.

As we sat at breakfast, he began to ask me questions about my business background, my family life, and what I wanted out of life. I told him about my business, my family, and I shared with him how I wanted to do a work for the Lord. When we left, I paid for our steak, eggs and hash browns and left a nice tip for our waitress. I slipped two twenties in his hand. I didn't set out to do this, but I have always been a giver to what I felt was God's work. I was only trying to bless our preacher, but when he saw me, he saw dollar signs. By this time, we had invited him home for dinner, so he had seen our house full of nice furniture and our well-dressed children.

On the last day of service, he asked me to meet him for lunch because he wanted to talk with me about my future. I was curious when we sat down to talk, so I listened as he told me that he pastored a beautiful brick church in San Antonio. He said his church had an attendance of 200 to 300 each Sabbath. He said he lived on a ranch with horses and cattle about 30 miles outside of San Antonio. Then he began to tell me how he could use a man with my abilities in his church and that I could live in a house on his ranch and work with him in the ministry as his assistant pastor. He asked me to think over and decide if I wanted to work with him in Texas.

For me this was a dream come true, so a week after he left, I sold and gave away my furniture, bought a small pop-up camper, loaded my motorcycle and we took off for Texas. When we arrived at the church, they were in service so we went in and listened to him preach. After the service, he came up and hugged us and introduced us to his family and congregation, then told me to follow him to his home. It was nighttime when we got there, and he had to get out of his car and open a locked gate so we could pull in. He pointed to an area under an oak tree and told me to pull in there so I could plug in. Mine was a cheap pop up camper so I didn't need to plug in. We removed my motorcycle and popped up our camper and went to bed.

The next day we got up to find them gone so I looked around. We were sitting out in a pasture with a mobile home, an old house, a small barn that was more like a shed with one milk cow, and one mare horse with her colt. The trailer was sitting under the oak tree and that was his ranch. I was devastated and felt used, but I've always been one who can make my way out of nothing, and I know now that I can contribute this to God's leading and His mercy.

When Bro. Dave came back from San Antonio, he asked me what my plans were. The dollar signs were gone and now he saw me as a burden. I began that very day trying to help around there so we at least were helping to make our way. His wife began to use my wife as a maid; we weren't put up in a house and I never saw his pulpit except from the audience. We slept in our pop-up camper at night, but during the day I'd ride my motorcycle to San Antonio to try to find a job. We drove to San Antonio on the Sabbath to go to his church, but people began to treat us like we were freeloaders; it was obvious that word was getting around that we were living off of Bro. Dave's good nature.

I was troubled because Bro. Dave lied to me in South Carolina when he thought I had money. But I believe God helps those who can't help themselves and I was at my wits end. I went to a plant called Underwriters Laboratory that sits on a multiplex in San Antonio and was hired the first day I applied for a job. People try for months to be hired there. When I told Bro. Dave I had gotten a job at Underwriters Lavatory he did everything but call me a liar, telling me, "Listen, if you are just leaving each morning to not be here, and really aren't working, I'll find out."

I said, "Well, if you'd like to follow me to work you

can, I don't mind." They started treating me a lot better when I came home to my family in a white U.L. smock with my name on it.

The next Sabbath a man came up to me after the service and asked if he could he talk to me. We followed him to his car. He said his name was Bro. G. from Nixon, Texas, where he pastored a church. He said he'd seen how Bro. Dave and his followers were treating me and my family and told me if I wanted a way out, he would rent me a trailer in Nixon and let me move into it. Nixon was about 50 miles from San Antonio. I told him we'd be there as soon as I drove to Bro. Dave's and got our camper. We left for Nixon that day. Bro. G. seemed concerned for us, but he also had an ulterior motive too, because even though both of them followed Bro. T's ministry, he and Bro. Dave were in competition with each other. We were put into a small one-bedroom trailer that rented for $10 a week, and Bro. G. asked me to give him my camper to compensate him for the two weeks rent he had already paid.

The people who rented the trailer were good and kind, and soon we'd become like family to them. There were two other trailers and a house on the two and a half acres they owned. They lived in one of the trailers and once they met us, they moved us into the other mobile home which was much nicer. I was 32 years old at that time, about the same age as their eldest son who worked as a roughneck drilling on an oil rig. He told me the rig needed a motorman and said he would teach me what I needed to know. Then I could tell the man who ran the rig that I was experienced.

We went to the man's home and he was satisfied I could handle the job so he hired me. The motorman's job was simple. He kept oil in the motors and greased the motor joints. He also had to help keep the mud at a constant level. Working on a big oil rig is very dangerous and quite a task with drilling a mile or two down into the earth to hunt for oil and gas. We were paid four times the hourly minimum wage plus a per diem of $75 a day for expenses to whoever drove. At 4 a.m. each morning we would drive 100-200 miles one way to get to work at 7. We'd relieve the night crew, work for eight hours, then be relieved by the next crew and drive back home. We slept going to work and coming home. We usually got home at 6 or 7 p.m. and we worked seven days a week. Once we hit oil and capped the well, we had a few days off until our site and rig were moved and set up again.

I was making more money than I could spend, but after a month I began to hate the job because I missed being home with my kids. Two months later I quit so I could be with my children at night.

I ran an ad in the newspaper for Jim's Roofing and Painting Service. A man who owned a house at the end of Main Street needed a roof put on so he called me when he saw my ad. His roof was an 8 x 12 pitch which meant it was steep and none of the subcontractors in the area wanted to tackle it. Since his home was on Main Street everyone in town saw me working. Soon my phone was ringing all the time and before long I was able to buy conveyers for putting shingles on the roofs and an airless painting machine for painting houses. I soon had to hire a crew and a foreman. I had a good business and was making enough money to put a down payment on my own home and furnish it with new and antiqued furnishings. I had a deep freezer full of beef, pork and chicken. I had built a building in my back yard so I could paint cars. I'd buy an older car that had a good motor and tranny, pull it into my building, put a coat of paint on it and sell it at a decent price.

I was making money and doing all the things I loved but had stopped going to Bro. Dave's or Bro. G.'s church and after a year I was depressed again. My soul was hungry and I was troubled all the time, so I bought a Chevrolet, fixed the fender and painted the car. My family got dressed up and we drove to San Antonio to Bro. Dave's church. We made quite an appearance when we pulled into the parking lot on the Sabbath before the service. We were welcomed with open arms by everyone this time and I felt at home in church again. Bro. Dave asked us to eat with him at a local restaurant. After we ate, I paid the bill, left the waitress a good-sized tip and slipped a $100 bill in Bro. Dave's hand. For the next year we attended his church and would go to IHOP on our way home with the Bro. Dave's family where I'd buy our meals. He began to come visit us in Nixon.

During that year, Bro. T. came for a weekend service. When Bro. T. came into an area people came from everywhere to hear him preach and minister to the sick so it was always hard to get a seat. But Bro. Dave always let me and my family sit in the reserved seat section up front.

Now life was almost perfect for me. My wife and kids were happy, whole, and being blessed and I worked hard every day so we could live a good life. But I had such a dark and gloomy past that I placed no value on material things, nothing lasted. I lived in the moment because the future always changed and I felt that I didn't belong anywhere and nothing belonged to me. The only thing that I had ever connected with was my children. I lived just to be with them.

Carolyn with their mom, Leila
and Jimmy, age 16 – 1962

Jimmy (left, age 22)
playing guitar with a
friend – 1967

***Jimmy (age 51) with
baseball trophy - 1997***

***Jimmy (age 53) with
daughter, Jennifer – 1999***

***David, Jimmy Jr., Billy,
Shelley, Jennifer***

Jimmy's Grandchildren
2003

Jimmy's 92-year-old mother.

Leila R Stroud – 2015

CHAPTER 17

One afternoon Bro. Dave came to my home and told me that Bro. G.'s wife was in the Cuero Hospital, so he was there to take him to see her and to pray for her. He asked if I would take his car, drive over to Bro. G.'s and pick him up. He said, "I'll sit here with Sister Sue and have a cup of coffee while you're gone."

I was gone maybe 15 or 20 minutes, and when I got back, I didn't go in because Bro. G. was in the back seat, so I blew the horn and Bro. Dave came out and got in the front seat. I drove through town headed for Cuero which was about 30 miles from Nixon. When we arrived at the hospital, we went to Sister G.'s room. After Bro. G. visited with his wife for a while Bro. Dave fervently prayed for her. Then we said our goodbyes, left, and I drove us back to Nixon.

I drove Bro. G. back to his home, walked him in, and then drove to my home. As Bro. Dave and I sat in my driveway, I asked him to come in and have a cup of coffee. Since it was already late and he had about 30 miles to drive, he kept refusing saying he really needed to go. But I insisted, so he finally came in. We sat in the living room and Sue brought him a cup of coffee. As we talked, I couldn't help noticing that Sue wasn't joining in, and when Bro. Dave stood to leave, Sue stayed a distance away. He was our pastor and we had always hugged whether coming or going, so I hugged him goodnight. But Sue walked out of the room. I said, "Sue, Bro. Dave is leaving. Aren't you going to say goodnight?"

She said goodnight over her shoulder and kept walking towards the kitchen. I saw him to the door and watched from the porch as he got into his car and drove off. I turned the porch light off and closed the front door.

When I turned around Sue was standing in our living room and this is what she said, "Jimmy, sit down. I've got something to tell you that is going to hurt you."

Instantly I knew! I said, "No Sue, not him!"

She said, "Yes, Jimmy, him!" She then told me what he had done when I drove his car over to Bro. G.'s house. She said he was at the kitchen table talking and drinking coffee and when she walked to the counter and turned around, he was there in front of her, had grabbed her and was trying to kiss her. She pushed him away and asked, "What are you doing? Are you out of your mind?"

He stepped back with an excuse saying, "Oh, I'm sorry. I'm just tired and I got confused for a second." She said almost immediately I blew the horn so he left.

I felt like my world stopped. I felt betrayed, confused, and I was getting mad. Sue asked me what I was going to do. She pleaded with me not to follow him home and confront him that night, but to sleep on it. But whatever I did she wouldn't blame me. I told her I would give him time to get home and I'd call him. I waited about 30 minutes. When he answered he was sniffling like he was crying. He instantly said, "Bro. Jimmy, I'm sorry."

I replied, "You know you hurt people tonight who believed in you."

He said, "Yes, and I'm sorry." Then he gave me his same excuse. He asked, "Will you forgive me, please?"

I said, "I'll try," and hung up.

I really did try to forgive him but at times my old "self" would start thinking about how he walked into my home and tried to commit adultery with my wife and then went to pray for a woman like nothing had happened. I wanted to tell everyone what a hypocrite he really was, but I knew that would only hurt other people. I could have been a troublemaker, but I asked him to drive back to Nixon because I had my offering to give him. I think that hurt him worse than if I had caused trouble. I didn't do it for him; I did it for me. If he had known the old me and what I was capable of, he wouldn't have tried such a sneaky thing. But I lived for my kids now and I wasn't going to let him cause my family more problems. However, I had lost all respect for him and the T. ministry.

After that, I stopped going to church. I started drinking and smoking again. I had put such confidence in Bro. Dave and the T. ministry, but now I couldn't believe in anything. Again, my world was shattered by someone I trusted, loved dearly and looked up to. I know people say we're not supposed to put trust in man, but we've all got our trust in men of character, and nobody expects their pastor to walk into their home and attack their wife. It just doesn't happen. I now knew that organizations had womanizers from the top on down and were greedy for money.

I was depressed so I decided to leave Texas. There was a preacher who I believed was a good man, so I told him he could move into my house and have everything in it since he had just moved there and was living in a trailer. As I said, nothing held any value to me and material things came and went all my life. I rented a U-Haul trailer, put my kids' bikes, toys, clothes and the rest of our possessions in it and left Texas for South Carolina. When we arrived at my Dad's house in Florence, I had bought a camper and a truck, so we slept in the camper and bathed in Dad's home. I began finding roofing jobs that I could sub contract from roofing companies in the area so I was able to feed my family.

A few weeks later I had enough money saved to rent a house over in Dillon. I went to a thrift store and bought a refrigerator, a stove, beds, living room furniture and eating utensils so we could begin to live a normal life. We enrolled our kids in school in Dillon, and when winter hit, the construction trade was at a standstill. I went to Walmart to apply for a job. Walmart always had a large turnover so I was hired in the sporting goods department as a salesman.

I began making a good living again, so I soon furnished our home with new furniture. I painted the house and put up storm windows and doors. When we moved in two years earlier, it was a cheap old wooden house with no paint, and it was so cold inside that you could see your breath. Back then the only heat we had was from the open oven door. But I fixed that old house so my kids could be safe and warm. I worked hard to give them a good life and home that I never had.

I was still troubled because of what I'd gone through in Texas. Sue and I rarely talked, only when necessary, and there was no affection between us. We were strangers sleeping in the same bed. I was dying inside and I needed to feel loved and wanted. We were living together just to raise our children. As I said earlier, I can't and don't blame her for anything I got myself into.

I began jogging and lifting weights so my body was well built. When working on houses, I worked with no shirt on, and I noticed young women watching me. Both single and married women began handing their phone numbers to me. Since I was getting no affection at home, I started having one-night stands.

While shopping for paint and rollers at Walmart, I met a young woman named Lynn. She asked questions about building materials, so I advised her on some things. Then she began telling me personal things about her husband verbally abusing her. I asked why was she telling me this and she said, "I have no one else to talk to and you are a good listener." So, I listened.

I gave her one of my business cards and told her if she needed any work done to call me. Early the next day while I was still in bed my phone rang. When I said hello, a sexy voice said, "I wish I could've seen the sun come up lying next to you."

When I asked, "Who is this?" she hung up. I thought about that all day long. When I came home, I took a bath and was sitting around the house when the phone rang. It was Lynn. I said, "It was you who called my house this morning, wasn't it?"

She changed to a sexy voice and said, "Would you like to see the sunset with me? If you do, meet me across the border at Howard Johnson's," then she hung up.

I dressed quickly and drove my van over there. She was sitting in a booth. I slid into the seat and we began to talk. Just then, as we gazed out the window, the sun was setting. She said, "Let's get out of here." I followed her car to an empty country house and parked under a tree. We committed adultery that night and for a month we met in North Carolina a few times each week.

We both knew the other was married. I had never asked about her home life, but one night she began telling me that her husband knew she was having an affair and he'd said if he ever caught us, he'd kill us both. I freaked out. Up to that point, I hadn't thought much about it. Since Sue didn't care what I did, I took it for granted that that was the norm. When I asked about him, she told me he was a highway patrolman in South Carolina. Instantly, I said, "Let's go!" When she got out of the van, I told her, "Don't call me, I'll call you." I ended the affair that night. I enjoyed being treated like a man, but the thought of dying scared me, and I wasn't going to die for a woman I didn't love.

Up to that point I had never been *in* love with any woman but Bonnie. The guilt and fear I was now living with was drowning me. I was so confused that I started going to a mental health center just to talk to someone. I didn't know which way to turn and I felt that all the churches and preachers were hypocrites and only wanted money, so I didn't trust God to help me get out of the quicksand I felt I was in.

The psychiatrist told me I was mentally ill because of how I was treated as a child by Dad and Clifton. He said I was a victim of child abuse and was fortunate that I hadn't committed suicide. I told him how my Uncle Gene whom I idolized and looked up to got tired of living one day, took a .25 automatic and put a bullet in his brain. He put me on a strong psychiatric drug that was supposed to help me sleep and balance out the mood swings that were getting worse.

I was only 33 years old and, instead of being happy, I was on a psych drug just to stay normal. The only time I felt any peace or happiness was when I was around my children. Everybody thought Sue and I were the perfect couple, but we seldom talked, and if we had sex, I had to initiate it. She wanted nothing to do with me. But, as I said, I didn't blame her because she knew I was a cheater. That didn't stop how I felt inside, though, because cheating feels good for a moment, but then the guilt starts.

I felt so guilty every time I looked at my kids. I wasn't only cheating and stealing time away from Sue, I was cheating on my kids. So, I decided one day when I was alone that I would go over to Marion where Bonnie and I used to park at a place called Blue Lake. I'd run a hose from the car exhaust into my window after taking a handful of sleeping pills and when I was almost asleep, I'd start up my car and go to sleep.

What saved me was I had run out of pills. I went to the mental health center to get another supply. But when I was telling the pharmacist what I needed, my psychiatrist came in. He said, "Mr. Windham, I'm glad you're here, because you missed your appointment and I need to talk with you." We went to his office and before long I was crying and telling him what I wanted to do. He told me I could allow him to commit me to a mental institution in Columbia where I could rest and get help. When Hal's wife was killed in the car wreck, Hal finally snapped and he was admitted to the institution where they gave him shock treatments. When he got out, he was like a zombie. So, when the doctor told me he wanted to put me in Columbia, I saw a picture of Hal and I said, "No way, Doc, I'll be okay."

I picked up my meds, took four pills, went home and went to sleep. I stopped making appointments with the doctor that day. Mentally I was messed up, but I decided that I'd go it alone. Looking back, that was a bad decision. I should've gotten all the help I was offered. If I had, maybe I would be fishing with my son Jimmy and my grandson Dylan instead of rotting away in a prison cell. Who knows? Only God!

CHAPTER 18

Shortly after that I kept noticing a beautiful young woman sitting on her grandma's porch. When I'd pass their house on my motorcycle, she'd wave and smile. One day, I went around the block, came back and parked my bike. Her young brother was playing with my kids in our back yard, so I called him over and asked why his sister looked so sad. He said it was probably because she had broken up with her boyfriend. I told him to ask her if she'd like to go for a motorcycle ride. He left and soon they came walking back.

Her name was Sherry; she got on and we left. It felt good, her body pressed against mine with her arms around me. We talked and rode all the way to Myrtle Beach. Once there we went into a sidewalk café and I bought her a beer. I had stopped smoking and drinking but she did both. As we sat there, she told me about the things she was going through with her boyfriend, and I began telling her about my problems at home. She said she couldn't believe it because everyone thought I had a perfect life. Before long we were crying on each other's shoulders. We finally left and it seemed she pressed even closer to me on the way home.

The air was cool, but my bike had a windshield fairing so we weren't cold. When we got to Marion, she asked if I would mind stopping to see her sister Wanda who lived with her boyfriend. Wanda was also beautiful. They talked for a few minutes and Sherry said, "Let's go."

Out by the motorcycle Sherry was having trouble with her chin strap so I leaned in to help her. I kissed her but finally pulled away. I said, "I'm so sorry. I shouldn't have done that."

But she said, "It's okay because I wanted you to." We got back on the bike and rode to Dillon. Outside of Dillon is a small roadside park where I pulled into it and we made lust on a picnic table. She may have been young but she was well experienced in pleasing a man and did things to me that my wife would never do.

Now this part of my story is heart-wrenching because I broke the hearts of my four innocent children, and I don't deserve their love or forgiveness. For the next three months Sherry and I snuck around to see each other, and I had fallen head over heels in lust with her. When I got off of work I'd come home, take a bath and go meet Sherry and sneak out of town. I wasn't home with my kids anymore, and it never dawned on me what I was doing to them. But those precious children are wonderful adults today.

Shelley was 14, Jimmy 12, Billy 10, and David was 8 but I left them to the wolves. Sue was not strict, and when she began to feel me leaving her emotionally, she started smoking and drinking coffee and not eating. She didn't know what to do, so my kids started doing as they pleased.

Can I blame all my failures on my brother Clifton? On my Dad? On my pastor? No! I blame my failures from this point in my life on my own selfishness. I blame me and there hasn't been a day that I haven't had to face my failures and the awful pain of missing my children. I'm reaping what I sowed because I left them when they needed me most. Thank God children don't hold on to pain like adults, and they readily forgive or they wouldn't want anything to do with me today.

One evening Sherry told me she wasn't going to be seeing me again. Her mom told her I had it made because I was sleeping with her and my wife. I told her I wasn't sleeping with my wife and that I loved her. Imagine telling her to stop seeing me because I'm sleeping with both of them, instead of because she was wrecking a family. I do accept responsibility; however, she had a share in it too. She said if I loved her, then I would leave my wife. I told her I couldn't leave my children because they were all I had until she came into my life.

So, for the next three evenings to make her point, she withheld sex. Believe me I know how Samson felt when Delilah told him "if you loved me, you'd tell me where your strength lies." All my life my kids were my strength, but I slowly gave in to her telling her okay, I'd leave my wife. Instantly she was in my arms. The next day I hooked up my camper to my car and pulled it into to a camper park and set up house with her.

At first, I could justify this because I'd go by my house every day to check on my kids and they seemed okay and didn't seem to be mad at me. Bear in mind that I was a strict but loving parent who watched over them. Once I was gone, they had freedom to do as they pleased, so they liked this arrangement. Things began to change though because Sherry was an alcoholic who wanted to fight after a couple of beers, and fight we did. She'd slap me and I'd slap her back. Slowly I started drinking and doing drugs with her.

Visits to my kids became fewer, because Sherry would accuse me of going home to see my wife. Sue would beg me to come back, and I wanted to, but I wasn't strong enough to break away from Sherry, the drugs, the drinking, and the sex. They were the strongest pull I've ever had in my life. I was a mess.

Then Sherry would start drinking and run off. It was common for me to hunt for her all night. When I found her, she would have hickeys on her neck. We fought all the time because of her running around. We would fight for hours, and in the next minute we were tearing each other's clothes off. If ever there was a fatal attraction, this was it. When she was drunk, she would tell me what a great lover her boyfriend was, and I would always say, "Well, if he is so good, why do you keep coming back to me."

Once after looking for her all night, I went home to Sue. She held me as I cried and told her how this girl was killing me inside. I told Sue how she would leave and come back with hickeys on her neck, smelling like sex. Sue begged me to come home. Suddenly, a neighbor was banging on the door saying, "Jimmy, your car is on fire."

I ran outside to see my car engulfed in flames. The fire truck put out the fire. After everybody left, I saw Sherry about two blocks down the street under a light. She yelled, "How do you like fire?"

I ran down there with intentions of slapping her around, but I said, "Sherry, you didn't have to torch my car."

She answered, "You didn't have to sleep with your wife."

The argument continued until we were pulling each other's clothes off. Then the fight started again because she had hickeys on her neck. Her boyfriend was intentionally provoking me. She got bold with her cheating knowing I would always take her back.

I had a friend named Mike who stopped by my camper one night. We sat outside on my car's hood (I had bought another car) listening to music, smoking drugs and drinking. I went inside to use the toilet and when I came back, she went inside.

Mike said, "Jimmy, listen. When you went inside, Sherry told me she wanted to have sex with me."

I said, "Mike, you're kidding me."

He said, "No. But she said she wanted you to join in."

I told him to go for it because I really didn't think that she was that evil. When we went inside, she was lying on the bed with the lights out and no clothes on. He undressed fast and got on top of her and penetrated her. I turned the light back on and was standing there with a butcher knife in my hand.

I told Mike, "You better leave."

He got dressed and left. She came off the bed and attacked me. I punched her, and she fell back onto the bed. I was so mad I grabbed my .22 Magnum rifle and shot twice just over her head. I wanted her to jerk up so I could shoot her, but she was out. When she came to, she shot past me and ran out into the middle of the road. I followed her and was trying to get her in the car when a highway patrolman blue-lighted her. He asked if I knew her and I said, "No, I was trying to get her out of the road," so he turned his attention to her. He cuffed her and took her to jail for public drunkenness.

The next morning, I drove my motorcycle to the jail to check on her and her daddy was inside making her bail. I waited under a tree on my bike when two preachers walked up and one asked if they could talk to me for a moment about my soul.

I said, "I'm fine but maybe you could talk to my girlfriend. She needs you."

They walked away and went into the jail to talk about souls to any inmate who would listen. I felt like I didn't have one because I lived in so much sin and guilt. I didn't think God would ever be able to help me. How many sane men would walk away from their children for a woman who cheated all the time? Little did I know that the worst was yet to come. Sherry had started telling me that her lover knew about me and had told her he was going to kill me. I was getting paranoid.

I had a .38 Derringer over and under, two barrels stacked, that I began to carry around in my shirt pocket just in case I ran into him, because she told me that he carried guns. At that time, I didn't even know who he was. All I knew about him was she kept bragging about his body parts and what a great lover he was. That really didn't bother me because I am a man too, but I was bothered that he wanted to kill me. I was more afraid of death than most people. The psychiatrist had told me that my fear of dying came from being scared that Clifton would beat me to death like he did that kitten. Whatever it was, I began to be scared of a man I had never met.

It was the weekend. I painted a house for a man, so Sherry and I drove to Florence to play pool and drink. I could tell Sherry was past her two-beer limit because she always got loud at that point. I tried to slow her down by not drinking along with her. I still had beer in my bottle when she would say, "Buy me another beer."

I would say, "Let me finish mine and I'll order us

both one."

Sherry began flirting with a man at the bar, so he told the bartender to give her a beer. I spoke up and told him, "If she gets a beer, I'll buy it."

For the next 30 minutes, she kicked and cussed at me saying, "Why don't you just leave. I don't want you. I want him."

Something inside me snapped. I told myself, if he comes around that bar, I'm going to shoot him and her. She would kick at me again and again, so I just looked at her and I was thinking, "I'm going to kill you tonight." I was no longer sane. She had humiliated me so much and had pushed me over the edge. I gave up my home, my children and everything I was, for her, and she humiliated me.

She verbally and physically abused me so she could have sex with a stranger. All I could think of was killing her. When that man saw I wasn't leaving, and maybe something in my face told him not to confront me, he left. Then she began to act nice, so we drank a few more beers. I would look at her and smile, but inside I was thinking, "I'm still going to kill you."

The bar closed at 1:00 a.m. and we walked across Palmetto Street to the Carolina dinette and I bought her breakfast. I asked her one question and other than that, we didn't talk.

I asked, "Do you know what I gave up to be with you?"

She said, "You didn't give up anything."

I said, "Yes I did. I gave up everything."

She smirked as she said, "You gave up nothing,"

I smiled and said inside, "Tonight you'll pay for calling my children nothing." I was numb inside and she was looking into the eyes of a man who had snapped.

Once she ate, we walked back over to R.L. Club's

parking lot, got on my bike and drove away. I was on Highway 76 out of Florence, headed towards Marion, when a highway patrolman got behind me. I made sure I didn't do anything wrong, and when I got to the Farmers Market, I put my signal on and turned left towards I-95. He stayed behind me for another mile or so and then shot around me. Once I got on I-95 I headed north; when I got to the Big Pee Dee River Bridge, I eased over and stopped. I got off my motorcycle and I slapped her so hard she toppled over backwards and dropped the helmet. I picked her up and slid her over the edge of the bridge. She was screaming, "Please, I'll never do that to you again."

I was holding her by her legs and just before I almost let her go, she said, "Jesus, please forgive me."

I pulled her back up and said, "if you ever treat me like that again, Jesus won't save you the next time."

Again, she said she was sorry. But when I exited I-95 and stopped at the red light, she jumped off my bike and took off running across the street towards a convenience store, helmet and all. I yelled at her, "if you get your boyfriend on me, I'll kill him tonight." She didn't see me when I pulled into a closed gas station across the street, as it wasn't lit up. I sat there watching her as she dialed the sheriff's office. Soon a deputy arrived and I could hear her telling him how I had assaulted her and threatened to kill her boyfriend.

The officer asked her, "Where does your boyfriend live?"

She said, "At the Palmer Motel, Room #7."

He backed out and took off in that direction. Once he was gone, I got on my bike, turned right towards town, but as I pulled out, she could see me. I said, "Not tonight. You won't get me that easy."

CHAPTER 19

I left and went to Sue's house and she let me sleep on the couch. I stayed at Sue's for three days and nights. She cooked for me, washed my clothes and treated me nice. I had been gone for seven months and things weren't the same with me or Sue.

One day the phone rang and I answered it. A man asked who I was. When I told him, he hung up. I asked Sue about it and she said he was only a friend and there was nothing going on between them. I still got mad and left. When I got to my camper, Sherry wasn't there but I saw her sitting in a bus a few lots over, so I went over. Two men lived in it and one of them opened the door. They were all drunk and she only had her bra and panties on. I asked her if she was staying there, but she said "no," and got dressed. She followed me to my camper, and we went inside. We didn't fuss, or argue over what had happened. We just went to bed and went to sleep. I was too emotionally drained to argue, but believe me, the next day we had a knock-down drag-out fight. She had hickeys on her neck, so I accused her of sleeping with Room #7, and she accused me of sleeping with my wife. We got louder and louder when a loud banging came on my door.

I opened it, and there were the two men who lived in the bus. They began threatening me and asking Sherry if she wanted them to beat me up. With a smirk, she told them, "No, I can handle him."

One said, "Well, if you want to come back to our bed, you know where we're at," and they left.

She told them she could handle me because she had seen me reach in my shirt pocket and take out my little Derringer and cock back both hammers; so she knew I was ready to shoot them both. That time she saved them. She was nervous because she had already experienced my rage, as it was only a few days earlier that I swung her over Big Pee Dee River Bridge to drop her. She talked softly now and said, "Let's just go get a beer and talk so I can calm down."

We got back in my car and went to a little bar over in Marion and started drinking. We were dancing and doing fine until I kissed her on her neck and saw the hickeys. I started fussing at her, so she said, "Come with me."

We went outside behind the building and rolled a joint and smoked it. Then she reached into her purse and took out a small bottle of pills and asked me to take one. I was at a point that I didn't care what happened, so I took it and chased it down with my beer.

We went back inside and sat down at a booth and instantly it was like cool water poured all over me. I felt such peace, so I asked what she had given me. She said it was Valium. I hadn't taken them before, but said, "Give me another one," so she did. I was drinking beer, going outside to smoke weed, and taking Valium like it was candy for the next hour or so. Then the man who owned the club heard me tell some fellow I could sell him a joint if he wanted one. I wasn't a dope seller ever, but I told him that so he would quit asking me if he could smoke with me and Sherry. I was asked to leave his club, so we left.

We stopped at a small store up the road on Hwy. 76 owned now by an old friend of mine named Danny Ray. That store was the same store my uncle owned and I worked and boxed there when I was a kid. Now I think it is ironic that at that same store, where I learned violence, it erupted in me that night. I lost all reasoning and sanity, because again I was looking at the hickeys on this woman that I loved and for whom I had given up everything.

It seemed like I was in a dream where I wasn't in control. Things were happening, and I was only watching. I had a small Case knife on my belt and I saw myself pull it out and stick Sherry with it. I couldn't figure out why she was laying on the floor screaming. Then I saw the woman who ran the store stick her hand in the door and yell something about the police coming. I was dreaming all this surely, and even though I was there, I wasn't able to control the dream. I had that bottle of pills in my pocket and a beer in my hand as I saw myself take a bar from the holders on the door and instantly, I was outside walking towards my car.

How I was able to drive to Dillon is beyond me because I don't remember driving there. My mind was fixed on Room #7 at the Palmer Motel. I had to get there and tell him to leave Sherry alone. I felt fear and paranoia when I'd think of him and his guns and that he wanted to kill me. In this dream I saw a friend's face as he handed me a .22 rifle. I remember stopping somewhere and buying a six pack of beer. I remember seeing a police car parked beside me as I sat there drinking beer and taking the rest of the pills. I remember waving at the policeman as I left, and I remember being in front of Room #7 with the rifle by the door. I remember telling a man I had never seen before that I needed to talk to him. I heard him tell me he had nothing to say about that whore, and I remember seeing a rifle in my arms, shooting. It was all a dream.

I remember driving to town and hearing a voice say, "You just killed a man," and I couldn't believe it. I was going in and out of reality. I remember turning around and driving back to the Palmer Motel. I saw an ambulance and a police car, and a lot of people, so I drove on past. I remember that voice saying, "See. I told you that you just killed a man for running around with Sherry," and I remember thinking about those two men in that bus, and I told that voice that I'm going to kill those men too.

How I got there, I don't know, but now I'm seeing myself driving into a gas station that is only less than a mile from those two men. I'm still in and out of reality, but more out than in; and when I was out, I would try to make myself come back down so I could figure out what was going on, and if this was really happening to me. I was all messed up. I had stopped at a station to buy another beer. When I pulled up, I saw five or six young men standing at the far corner of the station. I could tell they were smoking a joint because they were passing it around. I had pulled around past the pumps with the front of my car pointing towards the road. When I'd bought this beer, I had walked over to my car and put it on the front seat and then I walked over to this crowd of men. One was older and had a beard, while the rest were young. I said, "Hey, I see you all are smoking a joint. I'm all messed up, so will you let me get high."

The older man turned towards me and said, "I don't know you, man."

I said, "I know you don't know me and if it's money you need, I'll pay you."

He put his finger in my face and said, "I told you, man. I don't know you. You could be any M.F."

I said, "No. I'm not any M.F. But you won't ever forget this M.F."

I went to my car and got the rifle. When I walked up to them, I said," Hey, Big Mouth."

He turned around and I tried to hit him with the butt of the rifle. He jumped back so I began busting caps at the man, shooting him in the shoulder. The station was built on a hill above a big corn field and I as I turned to leave, I saw him rolling down the hill. When I got back in my car and started pulling out, bullets were spraying my car and busted out my side glass. I forgot all about the other two men and pulled onto the freeway and left.

I wasn't totally out of it then, but I was still going in and out of reality. I drove on I-95 until I got to I-20. Shortly thereafter, I couldn't drive because I was falling asleep, so I pulled off the freeway at Camden Exit beside a gas station and went to sleep.

I remember the car being shaken hard, which woke me up a little. I looked up and a policeman was standing in front of my car with his .38 pointed at me. Then I looked to my open door and another .38 was pointed at me. I was sitting behind the steering wheel in a deep haze like nothing was real. He said; "Ease your hands to your steering wheel, because if you move them anywhere but there, I'll blow your brains out. Do you understand me?" I thought I was still dreaming. Then I felt a handcuff hit my left arm, click closed, then he pulled me out of my car, and turned me around beside the car as the other policeman held his gun on me and finished handcuffing me behind my back.

I don't remember anything more until the next day when I woke up in a jail cell. I walked to the bars to look around. I had no idea why I was in jail but across from my cell was a man in another cell looking at me. I asked him, "What am I doing here?"

He said, "Man, they got you on a murder charge!"

I said, "You're crazy, who'd I kill?"

He said, "They say you killed a man over a woman."

Later on, that man tried to use me to get his sentence reduced claiming I confessed. I'm sure I didn't because I didn't even know why I was in jail until he told me, but that's how con artists like him do. I laid down and went back to sleep. It wasn't until two deputies from Dillon came to pick me up that morning, and after I was in the Dillon County Jail, I began remembering bits and pieces from all that happened the day before. It was like having a dream and trying to remember and all you get is bits and pieces. To be honest, I didn't want to remember it all because now I was in a real mess with no way to simply walk away.

CHAPTER 20

I was given a public defender named Mr. L. After two weeks, he told me he was sending me to Columbia for a two-week psychological evaluation, and I needed to try stay there as long as possible because the State was looking for aggravated circumstances so they could ask for the death penalty. My case didn't qualify, because to constitute as a death penalty case, there had to be another crime involved with the murder such as rape, robbery, or kidnapping. There was none, but the victim's family was prominent in the community and they were putting pressure on the prosecutor's office to go for the death penalty. My mental capacity at the time of the murder was not allowed to be presented in court.

In Columbia two psychiatrists who examined me said I was mentally unsound to stand trial, and at the time of the crime I was diagnosed with severe schizophrenia affective disorder which meant I couldn't relate to reality and schizophrenia paranoia which meant I was scared of everything. In order to determine that I was capable of standing trial, Dillon County disregarded the two psychiatrists' examination and brought me back to Dillon. They had a Dr. S. and an intern from the mental health center come to the jail to ask me who was the President, what day of the week was it and what was my name. When I answered those questions correctly, they determined I was capable to stand trial. None of this was presented at trial by my State-funded lawyer.

Prior to all of this I was in the county jail awaiting trial and to be sent to Columbia for the evaluation I just mentioned. All my life I ran from God and would get just enough religion to feel okay for the moment, but here I was in jail where I felt like a trapped animal. I was put in a cell used for people who needed to be protected. It had no bars like other cells but only a one-foot square Plexiglas window in the door. I was scared to death. I couldn't sleep and I couldn't eat. When I would fall asleep, I'd have terrible nightmares of people with guns or knives chasing me trying to kill me and I'd wake up in a cold sweat or screaming. I had even tried to pray for forgiveness; but when I prayed, I felt like He didn't hear me or didn't want to hear me. I felt like I had sinned too much for him to forgive me. I felt damned if I did pray and damned if I didn't.

Every three days I was given a shower. I had been given two changes of clothes by Sue so I could at least try to stay clean. When it was shower day, I was given a razor to shave with. But I had to always turn it back in so I wouldn't cut myself.

My case was high profile because of the victim's family. If my crime had involved a poor white man or a black man, the solicitor's office would have offered me a deal to plea to manslaughter (which is what it should've been). But because of who was involved and

146

because I had no money for a real defense, I wasn't given a chance to have a real trial.

On Wednesdays and Sundays, we would get a 10-minute visit from our families. My mom, Carolyn, Clifton, Sue, and my kids came to visit me. Sherry also showed up and Carolyn took her outside to ask her didn't she think she had done enough damage so Sherry left.

I had prayed and prayed night and day, but I couldn't find any peace. I was scared to death, I couldn't eat or sleep, and I was being threatened that the State was going to put me in the electric chair.

One day in the shower there was a razor someone had forgotten, so when I was done, I handed the jailer that razor and kept mine hidden in my towel. Back in my cell all I thought about was ending my life. I started planning it right then. I knew right after we showered the cook, Eddie Bracey, and Ron would come around hollering chow time, so I planned to wait until after he fed everyone so I wouldn't be caught.

I waited until night time. I got on my knees first and I started telling God again that I was so sorry for my crimes and my sins. I was so broken up as I prayed, I cried like a little child and told God, "I'm going to come to you soon and I hope you'll understand why I can't go on living. I'm more scared of those people wanting me dead than I am of you. So, please forgive me." That's how I felt and that was how I prayed.

I stood up and started cutting slowly into my wrist with the razor. It stung so I didn't cut deep because of the pain, but I'd cry and beg forgiveness for a minute and then cut some more. I hadn't hit my vein but I was bleeding a lot.

The old jail I was in had a set of bars as a door at

the end of the hallway and when the jailer would come onto the wing you could hear those bars clanging as they opened. Just then I heard them clanging. I looked out my window and saw the jailer and two men coming through the door. I hurried and wiped the blood off on a washcloth and put my sleeve down just as my door opened. The jailer said, "These men want to talk to you, can they come in?"

I said, "Yes, I guess so. What is it you want?" The jailer closed the door and left. One of those men was a preacher named Hayward Proctor, the very preacher who two or three months before as I sat outside the jail on my motorcycle as Sherry made bail for public drunkenness, had asked me could he talk to me about my soul. Now he was looking at a scared, confused, broken man who had nowhere to run and who an hour later would have met his maker because I couldn't go on living. I was more scared of living than I was of dying at that moment.

He looked me in my eyes and I'll never forget his first question to me. He said, "Jimmy Windham, do you believe that Jesus Christ can forgive sin?"

I was serious when I said, "Well, I want to believe that and I'm trying to believe that but I just can't believe that He could forgive me for all I've done."

He said, "We were at a prayer meeting tonight and the Lord spoke and said, 'Don't wait, go pray with Jimmy Windham in jail right now,' so we didn't delay. We came to tell you that the Lord has heard your cry and has forgiven you and will lead you if you'll trust him." So, I got on my knees and these two spirit-filled men prayed with me. They laid hands on me as they spoke in the Spirit. I heard them tell Satan to back away from me, take his hand off me because I had a job to do for the Lord. They fervently prayed for me and I cried and repented to God for all I had done and when I stood up, I was full of the Spirit of God, and I knew things had changed because I believed God had done this for me. God sent these men because I was serious; I wanted forgiveness because I was genuinely sorry for my sins and not because I was scared. I knew I had been changed because I wasn't afraid to face my crime.

All my life I bit my fingernails almost into the quick, and the next few days I noticed I hadn't bitten them. I knew God had forgiven me and I promised Him that day that no matter what came, whether it be a death penalty or a life sentence in prison, I would live for Him and testify for Him.

Through prayer and studying the Bible I got stronger, and four months later I stepped up to the bar and pleaded guilty to murder. I wasn't afraid anymore, I had truly repented and that day I made sure a reporter printed what I was about to say. I turned to my victim's family and with tears running down my face, I begged them to forgive me. I told everyone in the court I was so sorry for what I had done and the judge asked me had I asked God to forgive me and I told him, "I asked Him first."

The *Dillon Herald* has that recorded and I sent for a copy years later. I only had to tell them the day I was in court. The crime happened in October of 1984, but it was March of '85 when I went to court. Some of you reading this book even now, if you're interested, could call the *Dillon Herald* in Dillon, South Carolina, and get a copy to read. You'll see how God had truly changed my heart.

But I still had to go through the procedure and allow God to lead, because a few days after that I was taken to Central Corrections Institution in Columbia for my initial psychiatric evaluation. The state mental hospital on Bull Street in Columbia had a wing upstairs in one of the buildings at CCI where they housed men for a 14-day evaluation before their trial. I was there for three months because, as I told you earlier, I was diagnosed by two psychiatrists from the state hospital to have been schizophrenic before and during my crime.

I was in Stoney Building. There was only one way up and that was by elevator. The building area was square. The hallways had cells off to the right and in the center were day rooms and an old library. One corner in front of a day room was a partitioned-off area where men in white suits sat. When you walked down the hallway and turned right you were out of their sight. Then you'd turn right again, then right again before you'd be back around where they were. It was a mental hospital but, as I said, the rooms were cells with bars for doors.

The men in white were actually South Carolina Department of Corrections-hired and had no degrees, but there was at least one professional to pass out the psych medication. I was scared of that medicine so when they'd administer mine each day, I'd put it under my tongue and then flush it down the toilet. I was put in a cell off to the right near the front and close to the Technical Assistant's corner (we called them TA's), but the extreme mental cases where they yelled and hollered were kept penned up down at the end around the corners.

I started reading a Gideon Bible that I found, and would pray at night beside my bed. I was so taken by the life of David, and because his crimes paralleled mine so perfectly, I began to totally trust that if God had forgiven David for adultery and murder and called him a man after God's own heart, I knew he had forgiven me. I read Psalms 51 and it became the cry of my heart.

I knelt on a worn concrete floor where men had walked for a hundred years or more and I'd pray Psalms 51. I learned it by heart, it meant so much to me. Then I found 1 John 1:8-9. Verse 9 found its way into my memory and heart, and I'd confess my sins as it instructed, and I believed that He was faithful and just to forgive me of my sins and was cleansing me from all unrighteousness as it said He would. All the condemnation and guilt were being swept away by the words of life I was finding in the Bible. I noticed in John 3:17 God didn't send Jesus into the world to die for me to turn me away by condemning me. I was already condemned and guilty. I learned there that He sent Him to save me. All my life I never had a clue that someone loved me so much that He came to seek after me until I was found of Him and all my terrible sins could be covered and washed away by His blood. I fell in love for the first time in my life with Jesus Christ and the Bible.

We weren't given pens but were given pencils. One day I took my Bible, turned to Psalms 51 and I put each verse on the wall in a cloud that I drew. Then on the other wall I drew a cross with Jesus hanging on it, and under the cross I put I John 1:8-9. I was truly born again. As I said, I knelt beside my bed and I'd pray and read by prison yard lights for hours.

God's Spirit was captivating to me and I couldn't get enough. But one night as I was on my knees praying, I felt what seemed like a cat cross my legs so I looked up and in the light from outside I could see a sewer rat standing on his haunches looking at me before he jumped in my toilet to go wherever he wanted to go in prison. Believe me he was as big as a squirrel and from that night on I prayed up on my bed.

I was there about two weeks when I was asked to

help feed and clean up. Because I was a *runaround*, I wasn't locked back in my cell afterwards. I could go to the day room to play cards or ping pong with the other patients. I didn't play cards; all I wanted to do was find someone I could tell about my Savior. I'd walk the halls until I found someone who needed to talk. Since most of them stayed for only two weeks, I always had a new audience.

One day I turned the corner at the end and saw a man who refused to wear any clothes and who cried all the time. The T.A. said he was crazy but I had just read in one of the Gospels how Jesus met a man like that living in a cave and after Jesus prayed for him, he was then clothed and found sitting at the feet of Jesus. I asked this man, whose name was Jim from Frogmore, South Carolina, could I pray for him. I know it looked strange to the patients who passed by as I stood there holding hands with a naked man. But as I prayed, I commanded that evil spirit to go in Jesus' name and from then on when I passed Jim's cell, he was clothed and he would yell, "Come here, Bro. Jimmy, come pray for me and speak in that other language, because when you do, I feel God." He left shortly after that.

The Bible was becoming more alive to me every day and I was trusting God and had faith in Him that no matter what happened to me, I found in Romans 8:28 that it was for my good. I was no longer afraid. All my depression was gone. I found joy. My guilt was gone and I was happy to be alive. Oh, my sin is ever before me and I knew I'd pay to man for my crimes, and if I could trade places with my victim, I would gladly do it.

I was so wrong to let Satan use me to destroy my home, hurt my children and wife and to tear the heart out of a good family.

I can never make that right even if I paid for my crime in the electric chair. Nothing I can do could pay for what I put them through, but Jesus will heal their broken hearts if they'll let Him. He paid with a terrible death on a cross that belonged to me and He died to also take away their pain. But on both sides of this crime each individual must let Him be Savior. I'm not gloating in their pain, but I know by God there is forgiveness. If I'm never forgiven by man, it bothers me only for their sakes, because Jesus wants them to find a way somehow, someday in this life to forgive me; so for their sakes, He can forgive them of their sins.

Because I found God on my knees that night that Hayward Proctor prayed for me, and I repented with all my heart; God forgave me and gave me a promise of eternal life. I found in the Bible where God's word said no tongue would arise in the judgment and condemn me, because when God forgives us the record of our sin is wiped clean and can't be found. He promised you and me that He'd cast our sins away from us as far as the east is from the west and never to be remembered again. So how can anyone condemn us if God Himself doesn't remember what we did wrong once we truly repent of our sins?

Another instance that stood out to me as I walked around Stoney Building is that for a few days I passed a cell where I could see a man cowering in a corner by his window on the other side of the room. He had a long beard and long hair that was oily and matted. He had fingernails that looked like claws or talons that He'd have inside his mouth. As he clawed his mouth, blood and spittle would pour out onto his beard. He would stand there and cry so I'd stop and silently pray for him. At times I'd send down to the canteen and buy boxes of Tops tobacco. I'd let this one man who looked like a 60s hippie roll them and I'd hand them out to these guys locked behind their cell bars. One day as he was clawing himself, I stopped and asked would he like a cigarette. He went around the wall to get to the bar door and still hid behind the door, he stuck his hand out. I said, "Say Jesus." He went back around the wall to his corner. This went on for three days, but on the fourth day when he came around the wall and I said, "Say Jesus," his appearance changed and in a deep gruffy voice he said, "Satan is god." I was not expecting this. We hadn't talked at all and as he said that I felt an evil presence and without thinking about it all I could say was, "No, Jesus is God."

He said, "Satan won in the Garden of Eden," and I retaliated with "But Jesus won at Calvary."

He walked away, but for the next few days I'd stop and ask him if he would like a cigarette. He'd come around, hold his hand out so I'd say, "Say Jesus." One day He said, "Jesus," so I gave him a cigarette and lit it for him. I didn't smoke, but I was using it to try to help someone. Before he left there, I was praying with him and he asked Jesus to help him.

Shortly after that Dillon County came and got me and had Dr. S. determine me capable to stand trial so I was back in the Dillon County Jail. I witnessed to everyone I met about Jesus, especially to a man named Eddy because he was a trustee and came around to talk. He didn't believe me at that time, but a few years later at prison I received a letter from him and in it he said, "That Jesus you always talked about is now also my Savior."

Shortly after I arrived back this time I was put in a regular cell. One day a fine man named Dr. Thad Davis came to my cell. He said, "I heard you accepted Christ as your Savior before you left for Columbia, so I wanted you to know I also love the Lord and I'm your brother in Christ." Dr. Davis has been an inspiration to me and has stuck by me all 34 years of my incarceration. He would visit me there in the jail every few days and always bring me a box of Kentucky Fried Chicken. Even now if I need a friend to talk to or if I need prayer, I will call Dr. Davis and he will pray for me. His precious wife Jeanette also takes my calls sometimes and her sweet, kind voice always lifts me up as she prays for me.

Both of the Davis's have been such an inspiration to me and I owe them so much. Dr. Davis visited me many times in the various prisons I was sent to and was instrumental in helping me get approved for a better custody level. I want them both to know what a blessing they have been to my life. Dr. Davis has stuck closer to me than a brother. God bless you, Dr. Thad Davis.

Soon, my lawyer came to me in the county jail. He said, "If you plead guilty, they won't seek the death penalty and you'll save your family the embarrassment of a trial."

I said, "You know I didn't premeditate with malice aforethought to commit murder. I was out of my mind and on so many drugs, there's no way I planned this crime. This was a crime of passion and I should be found guilty of the lesser offense of manslaughter."

He said, "You're right but the Bennett family won't let the solicitor accept a plea except to murder." He said, "If you plea to manslaughter you'll be eligible for parole in ten years and with your work credits you'd be eligible in seven years, and if you plea to murder you'll get a ten-year life sentence and with your work credits you'll cut it down to seven years for parole eligibility." Either way would be the same.

I thought it over and decided that his argument

made sense and I had five months to get to this point. I had already repented before God with all my heart so I wanted the opportunity to openly confess the Lord Jesus. For five months, I was in the headlines every week for every little thing I did, so the day we went to court I wanted to make sure there was a reporter there and I asked him to please print what I was about to say. He assured me that he would, so in a broken heartfelt cry for forgiveness I repented in open court. I was so broken up as I turned to the Bennett family and begged them to please forgive me until Fred, the brother of the victim, came and hugged me and told me he forgave me. He's had a change of heart since then because, even though I've done everything possible to show rehabilitation, he appears against me each year at my parole hearing. We ordered the tape one year of the hearing and he said he'd never forgive me.

Anyway, I pled guilty and after the usual questions and answers with the judge he gave me the mandatory life sentence for murder. I was out of my mind due to all the drugs Sherry gave me, and that mitigates intent – premeditation, malice aforethought. I'm guilty of a crime of passion -- manslaughter. There was no justice in my case, but I've grown to know the Lord so I know if He wanted me free then somehow, someway, He'll make it possible.

When we got back to the jail there were so many things running through my mind. I wondered how I would be able to do a life sentence. I worried night and day for my children and I wondered how a Christian could live around the most violent men and it not affect his thinking. The only thing I knew about prison was what I had seen on TV so I was overwhelmed with fear, anxiety, and depression.

CHAPTER 21

After our court appearances we were handcuffed to each other and put into a van that took us to the Receiving and Evaluation (R&E) center. The van didn't have seats, so I was sitting on the spare tire handcuffed to a man on my left and on my right. They had my arms stretched over and dangling because they had their wrists on their knees. I thought how could a Christian be passive in prison? Being a fighter all my life I thought I will need to defend myself so I roughly pulled their arms loose and placed my wrists on my knees so I would be comfortable.

When we arrived at the R&E center in Columbia, we were examined, x-rayed, had blood work done and given shots. When I was examined by the psychiatrist, he asked me "Do you hear voices?"

I answered with as honesty as I could. Because I was studying the Scriptures, I knew God spoke to us in His Word so I openly said, "Well, the Lord speaks to me."

He instantly sat up and said, "Does he tell you to

hurt yourself or others?"

I then realized what he meant, so I tried to correct my error by telling him, "No, sir, and anyone who reads the Bible can hear God's voice."

When we got back to our cells two men in white came and said, "Jimmy Windham come forward." I reluctantly stepped through the bars and one of them handcuffed me. It's not something you ever get used to, it's devastating to be sure. You already feel helpless and when you're handcuffed, you are powerless to lift a finger. One minute I was lying on an old iron bed and the next minute they were taking me to an unknown location because I had said God speaks to His people.

We were driven across town to Kirkland Correctional Facility. Many gates opened and closed behind me, and I saw miles and miles of Concertina razor wire. I was driven to the back of a building called The Gilliam Center, a mental hospital for South Carolina Department of Corrections (SCDC).

Inside I was led off to the left of a control booth that had bars and glass all around it. There were rooms upstairs and downstairs with only a small 5-inch by 2-foot window in the steel doors. Men were yelling and beating on their doors as I was led upstairs and placed in a room. There was no furniture in the room, only a concrete block area with a thin mattress. The room had a stainless-steel toilet and sink where you had to push a button to get water. At the end of the bed was another 4-inch by 2-foot window, but all I could see was yellow lights on 50-foot metal poles and fences with razor wire at the bottom and top of the fence.

I realized that even if I could get past the control booth and outside, there was no way to get over those fences. I was trapped in a world of fences and razor wire. If I screamed no one would come because I was in a mental hospital where someone is always screaming. There were no books, no pen and paper and no phone; the real world was gone; it was as though I didn't exist. I prayed like I've never prayed before. I told God how alone I felt and I cried and cried as I told Him how I missed my children and begged Him to take care of them. With tears running down my face I looked up and said, "God, this can't get any worse, and I can't do a life sentence in hell."

About that time, I heard a knock and there stood a man in white who motioned me to the door. He asked, "Why are you crying?"

I said, "Because I'm praying."

He said, "I pray but I don't cry."

I replied, "Well, you're not in my shoes." He left.

Never tell God it can't get worse. My door opened and two more men in white asked me to come with them. They took my clothes and put me in a cloth gown. The room had a bed under a camera so they could watch my every move and the mattress weighed at least 100 lbs. Believe me, it got worse.

That next week my clothes were returned and I was taken to the psychiatrist. I told him why I was there, that I wasn't crazy and asked him how to get out. He described the three-step plan I would have to go through. Each step lasted a month or more depending on my progress.

Step one: I had to eat meals in my room and once a day I could go outside to a small fenced area for fresh air and sunshine. This gave me a chance to mingle with other inmates.

Step two: I could go out into the yard with the inmates, but had to come back in to eat lunch and dinner in my room and then I could go back outside.

Step three: I could leave my room in the morning

and go out into the yard. I could eat lunch and dinner in the cafeteria. I could go to the canteen or I could lift weights, go to the rec field and play horseshoes or soft ball. Life was looking up.

I started attending the church services and singing in the choir. I began to grow in grace and in the knowledge of God's Son. I met other Christian brothers who lifted weights and we became friends. One brother named Ted left and went on to become a preacher. His pastor, Bro. Jim Dutton near Augusta, Georgia, was from a strong Word church; he took me under his wing by sending me cassette tapes of their services. At that time, I really needed his support.

I attended Bible study with Ted and a man named Sammy. The man who came to teach us that night was tall, about 6 foot 7 inches, and he drew his message on an easel board. As he'd tell about Christ teaching or walking down a road, he'd draw pictures of the scene. It was a good way to keep one's interest. A Christian brother named David Harmon came with him, and he said he could see an aura around me and he believed God had His hand on me. When he asked why was I in prison, I told him it was because of a murder charge over a woman. He then told how his wife had left him for another man and he almost was in my shoes. He laid hands on me and prayed. Afterwards he told me he believed it was God's will for us to become friends, so I thank God for Bro. David Harmon because we're still friends and he has stuck by me.

Bro. David still goes around in his spare time to jails to tell the prisoners about Jesus and His love. I've never known a man who cared more for the souls of inmates as Bro. David. God bless you, Bro. David. We'll be home together soon.

Because I officially hadn't finished my R&E time to be assigned to an institution and I was nearing the end of my Stage Three progress, I was advised by Ted and Sammy that I should ask the warden to help me be assigned to Kirkland since I had made friends and was in church there. I saw him shortly after that in the yard one day and I explained my situation to him. He told me to write it all down on a *Request to Staff* form and when I left to go back to the R&E center to drop it in his box and he'd see what he could do, so I did.

I was still in Step Three in the Gilliam Center when I began to lift weights. I kept seeing a young black man who also lifted but we never talked. I had been praying and asking the Lord to help me make a difference in somebody's life. When I went back to my room that evening instead of going to the TV room (because I had TV privileges) I felt led to stay in my room and pray. That young man's face kept coming before me so I seriously prayed for him. The next morning after breakfast I went out to the weight pile and only he and I were there. I told him, "Listen I know we don't know each other, but last night I was burdened to pray for you. Are you all right?"

He said, "A man tried to kill me with an ice pick last night, and the only thing that saved me was I had a string art board in my hand and he kept sticking it instead of me."

I asked if he was a Christian and he said no. I began telling him how Jesus saved me so he asked if I would go to his room and pray with him. On the way, we introduced ourselves. His name was Clarence from Columbia, South Carolina. On our knees, with tears running down his face Clarence gave his heart to serve Jesus Christ. Clarence stayed at Kirkland another year and during that time he got baptized and was totally dedicated to the Lord. I saw the change in him. He truthfully repented before God that day. He knew it was the Lord who caused me to pray for him and he knew it was the Lord who spared his life. Years later, Clarence was still coming to visit me.

While at Kirkland, I kept hearing about a man called Red Dog. I was told that he had been a vicious killer who would never get out of prison. They said he'd as soon kill you as look at you, so I thought, "Boy I want to meet him so I can get on his good side." They said he was red headed, about my height and lifted weights. I said, "I can't place him. The only person who I know who looks like that is a good Christian brother named Ronald, who when you ask him how he's doing, always says, 'One day at a time, brother, one day at a time.'"

I was told, "That's him!" Ron had such a change when Jesus became his Savior, it was like day and night. I heard later that Ron had gotten out of prison and was married to a wonderful Christian lady and they had a prison outreach ministry. I was even told that Ron was seen on TV witnessing for Christ. All I can say to Ron if I ever see him is, I took his advice and I learned to serve Jesus and do this one day at a time. God bless you, Ron, wherever you are.

I finally was released by the doctors at Gilliam Center and was to leave the next morning for the R&E Center. I wasn't sure if I would be transferred to Kirkland (K.C.I.), so that evening my Christian family gathered around and laid hands on me to ask God to use me for His glory wherever I was sent. We cried and hugged like it would be the last time we would see each other. I loved those men and prayed God would let me come back to K.C.I. to be with them. I'd also met a short black-haired man called T.D. who did me a lot of dirt. If he ever reads this book, I want to tell him, "I forgive you!"

As I lay in bed, God reminded me of that first night when I felt totally alone. Now I felt loved, loved by

God, loved by my friends and loved by my children who came to visit every two weeks. God was blessing me to make a difference in the lives of others. I had never felt this way before and, even though I was in prison doing life, I found that God is in control and that in itself made me feel secure that night.

CHAPTER 22

The next morning, I was handcuffed and led out the door into a van to be driven back to the R&E Center I had left three months earlier. I was going back a different man than when I left, I was growing in the Lord. Even the fences looked different. The razor wire was no longer scary, because when God has made someone free, they are free indeed; and a life sentence isn't as bad as it sounds when you have eternal life. Was I still struggling and battling daily? Of course. What real Christian doesn't, but I found strength coming from within where Christ lives.

When we arrived at the R&E Center on Lincoln Street I was ushered in and assigned to the block overlooking the yard. There were 10 cells with an eight-foot catwalk on our block. Outside the bars was a TV and windows that overlooked the yard. At the end of the catwalk was a community shower with four stations. In the mornings, a guard pulled the lever which opened all 10 cells in unison so we were free to leave our cells, watch TV, or take a shower. I began holding prayer meetings in my cell in the mornings and afternoons, and a lot of inmates came in at different times as we'd pray for them and their needs. God was moving and we began to get praise reports back on the prayers God had answered, so my faith was also growing. There were six men who were devout Christians who were always together sharing the Word and always willing to pray with others who had a need or wanted to be saved.

I met Don, a radio announcer, and he still had the charisma of a disc jockey. When Don finished reading a scripture, I sometimes would joke, "And now the weather." Don and I became friends, and when the cells opened in the mornings we got together for prayer, scripture reading, and a cup of coffee while the others slept in. Don was so in love with Jesus, his face and smile showed that light of Christ that was in him. I asked him how long he had been saved. I felt it had been a while because of his strong stand for the Lord and his deep love, but listen to what he had to say. This will bless you!

He said, "I've been saved for only a few months. I didn't know how to get saved, but I was put in a cell at Stoney Building at CCI for my 14-day psych evaluation. Somebody had drawn the 51st Psalm in clouds and on the other wall had drawn Christ hanging on a cross." I knelt down and asked God to save me.

I stopped him and asked, "And under the cross was I John 1:8-9 'If we confess our sins, He is faithful and just to forgive us of our sins and to cleanse us from all unrighteousness'."

He said, "You saw it too?"

I said, "Don, I wrote it over 6 months ago."

He said, "I confessed my sins that day and accepted Jesus as my personal Savior."

God once again showed me that even in my brokenness back then He had a plan for my life and He was leading me. Proverbs 3:5-6 tells us to trust in the Lord with all your heart and lean not on your own understanding. Verse 6 says to acknowledge him in all your ways and he'll direct your path.

It was hard to trust in God and to not try to figure out how I could do a life sentence. I could see the razor wire, I could see the fences, but I learned to turn loose of what I could see and trust in what I couldn't see. That is faith and without faith, we can't please Him. I found a scripture that said that he who comes to God must believe that He is and that He's a rewarder to them that diligently seek Him. The more I trusted God the more He moved, and the more He moved, the more my faith grew, and the more my faith grew, the more I would praise God for answering prayers.

God is not a man that He should lie or the Son of man that He should repent. If He said it, He'll also bring it to pass. We can trust God because He's in control, not the South Carolina Department of Corrections, not the governor, not a parole board. God is in control. Do I really believe that? Well, let me put it this way. I've been up for parole 11 times now. About five or six years ago I was getting ready to see the parole examiner but in prayer one night I told God, "I'm trusting in You. Not in SCDC or a parole board to set me free." I felt an unction inside me and two weeks later when I went to see the parole examiner, I told her I wanted to sign a refusal because I wasn't coming this time. She kept asking me why. I told her I have my reasons. When back in prayer again I told my Lord again, "I'm trusting You, not a parole board." Yes, I believe God is in control.

Shortly after that, I was told to pack up because I

was being assigned to another prison. I asked the C/O where was I going, and he said, "I don't know, you'll find out on the loading dock." At the loading dock, they had us wait till we were called and then told to get in line to board bus #1, #2, #3 etc. I was praying but I trusted God to send me where He wanted me. When they called my name, I was told to get in line #2. Once in line, I asked the inmate in front of me where was he going, and I was happy when he said Kirkland. God had answered our prayers again. I couldn't wait to see my Christian brothers at Kirkland. Even Don was going with me to K.C.I. and that made him happy.

When we arrived, we were taken off the bus and ushered into the Operations Building to be assigned our building and room. I was assigned to C-1-8. C-2 was a Gamon Dorm which means the inmates are more mature in their actions. I had a good room downstairs by the two wing doors. On the other side of the wing doors was where a man named Henry lived and Henry had a big canteen.

CHAPTER 23

Now, let me tell you about prison back then. There were gambling tables behind the buildings where inmates gambled for big money. There were drug sellers everywhere. Every building had small canteens run by inmates who invested their money in stock to sell at an inflated price. For instance, the inmate would buy sodas for 25 cents, ice them down and sell them for 40 cents. He'd buy cakes for 25 cents and sell them for 35 cents. The staff didn't bother him because that was just the way it was back then. Loan sharks would loan you $10 for $15 back in two weeks. Men went around selling clothes, jewelry, TVs and anything else you wanted. You could even buy a pint of whiskey for $25.

I was housed by the wing doors which was a perfect spot for a canteen. Back then we got State pay, so the yard always had money in it. An inmate with no habits could make good money. As I said, it was legal because that's just how it had always been. Because of my love and concern for my family, I started my own canteen. Even though I was in prison I still prayed for and tried to guide my boys. I had raised them to not rebel against me. When they visited, I still advised them and had one-on-one sessions with them. My sons are all fine men today because I tried to instill character in them.

I was so sorry for what I had done. But it was done, so we made the best of the situation. As a Christian and praying father, I asked God to help my family. I prayed that God would take care of my children, and I can witness for the Lord that it was He who kept them and led them. I took care of my family from prison.

Now, some of you may not like it and may judge me for it, but here's how I believe God answered my prayer. I was getting $10 state pay so I'd save it until Sue brought my kids to see me and I'd give it to her to help with gas money. One day a man asked if he could borrow it. He said he'd pay interest on it so I loaned it to him. $10 turned into $15. With it I bought 2 loaves of bread, mayo, ham, cheese and chips and some sodas and opened up a small canteen. Before six months I had the biggest canteen in the yard. I had four 48-quart coolers that were full of sodas, milk, and juices. I'd buy hamburger from the kitchen and I had a box built to hold an iron upside down that I kept covered in tin foil so I could fry or toast sandwiches. All the C/Os ate at my store.

Besides having the biggest canteen, I was loan sharking. I took in for pawn TVs, radios, new Levi jeans, coats, gold rings, and necklaces. Now what did I do with all that money? Every two weeks I would take in around $600 plus the gold some inmates lost in pawn to me. I gave my wife, Sue, half of it or $300 to pay her rent, the light bill, to feed my children and to pay for phone calls. I'd restock with the rest. I fed my children from prison. I put gold rings on my sons' fingers. I put gold around my daughter's neck and I would give my kids personal money for themselves. I bought my son's first automobile from prison. I bought their school clothes. Like I say you may think hard of me for loan sharking and selling sandwiches, but those inmates were going to borrow it from someone, and I can tell you that none of the loan sharks or canteen men were working for their families.

My son, David, came to visit me one day years later, and as I sat in front of him, I was telling him how wrong I was for leaving and I was crying as I said, "Son, I'm so sorry." He stopped me and said, "Stop it, Daddy. I'm proud of you because you didn't stay down, you turned to the Lord for forgiveness and guidance while most inmates turned to drugs. You sold sandwiches and sodas so I could eat while most inmates still took advantage of their families. So stop crying. I'm proud of you."

He also said, "While most inmates just run the yard you went to school to get your GED. You then enrolled in college, you took every social worker class you could take, you finished carpentry vocation school, you finished plumbing vocation, you finished auto body repair, and you finished welding. You made a 12.9 on the Test of Adult Basic Education (TABE) so you could be a teacher's aide in school to help men learn to read and write, then you went back and got your actual high school diploma. You did all this because you wanted to come back home to me one day. So, I'm proud of you, Daddy. No man could go through what you've been through and still have faith in God and faith in the system of SCDC that one day, because of all you've done to show what you're really made of, they'll let their system work for you."

In March of '86, I was in a social worker's class

called, *How to Improve Your Life.* I had already been to two of the required four classes and unlike most of those social workers classes that are boring, I was enjoying this one because the gentleman giving it, Mr. Bruton, was a Vietnam vet and told us a lot of his war stories.

So, on the night of April 1, 1986, as we were lounging around in our building, in the D block, which is the lock-up building, a few violent inmates captured the C/O, took his keys, and locked him in a cell. It's amazing how quickly a riot spreads, because that night SCDC would experience the most expensive and biggest riot they had before or since. Two inmates got out of their cells, went around and opened all the cell doors, so there were 150 violent troublemakers out of their cells burning and trashing the D building.

Once they got outside, violence began to spread to other dorms. When the C/Os on duty saw what was beginning to take place, most of them ran for Operations to get out of the prison. Mr. Bruton came running to my cell, so we locked him in with us. His office was in our building, and at one point he asked me to go see if his briefcase was still there. But when I went upstairs to look for it, I found his office on fire. The yard was full of inmates running around destroying state property. I started downstairs when I ran into two inmates from the D-Block who asked me if had I seen Mr. Bruton. I said, "Yeah, I saw him about an hour ago running for Operations." So, they left, hunting him to take him hostage.

I liked this decent man and I wasn't going to let anything happen to him. The building was filling up with smoke so we decided to dress him in prison clothes and get him out of there. He put them on and two more of my friends and I ran with him to Operations. Then we went to see if anybody needed our help.

We went to another building, where we recognized a C/O who had worked in our building but he was dressed in prison blues. We asked why he hadn't left already, and he answered he had been too scared to go into the yard. The yard had around 500-600 inmates near Operations because the canteen was near there, and they had broken into it. We told him to follow us and we walked him out. After the riot, we never saw him again because it scared him so badly that he quit.

On top of the Operations building there were C/Os in riot gear with rifles, but they weren't allowed to come in because they didn't know where or who their officers were. They only knew there were still officers unaccounted for. The thing is, God was in control of that riot, because not one officer or inmate got hurt and that doesn't happen ever in a full-scale riot. The prison itself was being destroyed, but no human life was taken.

In every building all the doors and windows were shattered. All the offices with their computers and furniture were set ablaze and destroyed. The library was the biggest and best SCDC had ever put together, and it was set on fire. This library even had little guinea pigs and hamsters so an inmate could hold and pet an animal, but the smoke and fire killed the animals.

Around midnight the warden announced that all inmates were to go to the rec. field because the riot squad was coming in and would forcibly put down any resistance. Everybody knew what that meant, they were coming to crack heads if you were still in the prison and not on the rec. field. All the inmates begin to slowly make their way to the rec. field, with the violent inmates who started the riot there among us.

Before the riot, we were lounging around in our

short pants and t-shirts inside a warm building. Now we were on a rec. field with the temperature dropping, so inmates started fires and began to burn whatever they could find. I saw the scoreboard being pulled down and go up in flames. Then some of the more violent inmates who started the riot began to go around hunting those they knew who had a canteen. When they found him, they'd rob him and take his jewelry.

When I saw this being done, I pulled off my wedding ring and watch and put it in my pocket just in case they picked me out. But, instantly, the Spirit of God put me in check and said, "That isn't trusting God," so I pulled it back out of my pocket and put it back on my finger and wrist. The robbers came all around me, but the Lord didn't let them rob me. Bear in mind, also, that I was already built up by working out on the weight pile every day, plus they knew of my background as a trained fighter. So, I'm glad God didn't let them come to me, because though they may have robbed me, it wouldn't have been easy.

Finally, around 4 a.m. when the riot was over and the C/Os were back in charge of the prison, we were taken out of the rec. field by dorms and I was so glad to get back inside to some heat. Because my room was downstairs and beside the wing gates, my room didn't suffer smoke damage like the rooms upstairs since smoke and heat rise. The men living upstairs really had to suffer for a few days until they could clean their rooms and get rid of the smoke smell.

A few days after the riot as I was walking down the sidewalk going to the canteen, Mr. Bruton was coming up the sidewalk going to our building. He stopped me and said, "Mr. Windham, I really want to thank you for what you did the other night for me."

I said, "Mr. Bruton, I didn't do it for you."

He said, "You didn't?"

I said, "No, sir, I did it for me."

He said, "How so?"

I said, "Well, you know I'm in your social class and I've already taken two of your classes, so I did it because I didn't want to start over." He smiled and hugged me right there on the sidewalk in the middle of prison. This wasn't a state employee and a prisoner hugging. This was two men who both loved the Lord and who just happened to be on different sides of a badge.

Shortly after that my faith was tested because the man who had a canteen beside mine told me I was stealing his customers. I told him, "Henry, there's plenty of money in this prison so don't be jealous of me."

He said, "Well, I'll put you out of business."

I said, "You didn't put me in business. The Lord did, so you can't put me out." Henry would use the "N" word a lot and wasn't as clean as I, so his customers didn't come to me because I enticed them, they came because they didn't like Henry. His main god was money, and the inmates knew that my money wasn't mine. I took in $600 every two weeks so when my wife brought my babies to see me, I gave her at least half and with the rest I would restock my store. When I told Henry that he didn't put me in business, but the Lord did, I meant that.

Unlike Henry, if someone charged at my store and couldn't pay me, I didn't get upset and go fight them. I'd go to them and tell them, "Listen, that money you owe me, I know you'll pay me when you get it, but don't go to someone else's store and spend your cash because you owe me. Come spend your cash with me and pay me this other when you can." I kept customers that way. God was really moving in my life.

When Henry made his threat, I didn't take him seriously. But a few days later, as my roommate and I were starting our day I noticed a weasel-looking guy in our building; he was from another building. Every time I'd glance at him, he'd look away. I was in a hurry to get to the canteen so I wasn't too concerned with him. My roommate, Jerry, and I left. About an hour later a C/O with contraband came up to me in the canteen line and asked me to come with him, so I handed my list and money to a man I had hired to work for me and I followed the contraband C/O. He took me to the captain's office. Outside the captain's office was a bench and Jerry was sitting there.

He said, "What do you mean by having a shank in our room?"

I said, "I've never had a shank."

He said, "Well, it isn't mine so it's got to be yours."

I said, "Jerry, I've never had a shank, and my God will vindicate me because He knows I'm telling you the truth."

The captain called us in and, sitting on top of his desk was a pointed six- or seven-inch piece of metal with tape on one end. He looked at Jerry and said, "Jerry, is this yours?"

Jerry said, "No, sir, Captain."

He looked at me and repeated his question, to which I said, "No, sir, Captain, I've never seen that shank before now."

Then the captain thought for a minute and he said, "Jerry, I believe you. And, Jimmy, I asked about you and was told you are a weightlifter, you don't smoke, do drugs, or drink. You attend church services and sing in the choir, so I believe you, also." Then he said, "Have you made anybody mad lately?"

Instantly I thought of Henry's words, "I'll put you out of business."

So I told him, "Well, Henry and I had a few words."

He said, "We'll watch your back."

The weasel guy had pushed the shank under my door when I left for the canteen, and Henry used a pay phone to call Operations to tell them I had threatened an inmate with a shank. When Jerry and I left the Captain's office, I told Jerry, "I told you my God would vindicate me." But as I walked hurriedly towards my building with all intentions of confronting Henry because my flesh was in control at that moment, the Holy Spirit of God began to move in me. I recently had read a scripture that said no weapon formed against you shall prosper and one that said you shall hold your peace and I'll fight your battle. "Because vengeance is mine, saith God, and I will repay." The fighter in me wrestled against God's Word in me, and here's what happened.

When I reached the bottom stair Henry, who was buffing the floor, stopped buffing and looked at me with a questioning stare. I made the decision to put God's Word first. I looked at him and in a loud voice I said, "The Bible says no weapon formed against me shall prosper!"

I went to my room, sat down on my bed, and held on to the sides of the bed and I said, "Dear Father God, you know me, you know that I fear no man, and you know right now I really want to go bust that man up. But you told me in your Word that if I'd hold my peace that you'd fight my battles. Well, Lord, this evil man has tried to take food out of my children's mouths and if it wasn't for your Word, I would hurt him, but I turn all of this over to You to judge. Amen." I gave it to the Lord and I left it there. In Psalms 91 the scripture says, "Only with thine eyes shalt thou behold and see the reward of the wicked."

A few days passed and I was standing outside of my

canteen waiting on my floor to dry. I saw Henry standing in front of his store with a wad of money two or three inches around. He had just counted it and put it in his shirt pocket, but a C/O walking up behind him reached around and took that knot out of his pocket, peeled off $50.00 (which was the limit we could have), and told him, "I'm writing you up for loan sharking." There were probably $2,000 or $3,000 in that wad. I thought about God's Word when I saw that.

Two days later I heard a commotion so I came out of my room to see a black man and Henry arguing in front of Henry's store. The black man was trying to reason with him. He owed Henry $45 (he borrowed $30) and Henry held his TV as collateral. He tried telling Henry he didn't get his visit so he couldn't get some money, but He'd get it next week. Henry told him "No, that TV is mine," and used the "N" word. That black man slapped him so hard and fast that Henry fell backwards. The man went into Henry's room, took his TV off of a shelf, and when he was leaving, he said, "You're paid!"

The very next day Henry was chased up front by five friends of that black man that came to see if he was man enough to call them by the "N" word. He was never seen in that institution again, because God put him out of business.

And that isn't all. His roommate called me that afternoon and said he had moved down to Henry's bed and kept feeling a lump under his foot so he looked and found a hole in the mattress. He pulled out a wad of $100 bills. He found over $2,000 of Henry's money. God keeps His word. Did I gloat over Henry losing everything? No! Years later when I was at Lieber Prison someone came and told me that Henry was in Medical, so I went to Medical to see him. He came outside with me, so I walked and talked with him. We even hugged each other when we parted. I would never want to see someone suffer because of me, but we all make choices in life, and we will reap what we sow. Henry was out of God's will and I was in it, so God used all of that to chasten and correct Henry. All un-repented sin will bring consequences to us.

CHAPTER 24

Before the riot, K.C.I. looked like a college campus with trees, flowers, and shrubbery. After the riot the prison looked drab and depressing, every building had black soot marks around the windows and doors.

One day in July 1986 a caseworker called me to her office; she said a new prison called Lieber was opening near Charleston and she needed a white barber to go and cut hair for staff and inmates. She asked if I would consider going. I had already heard through the prison grapevine that the Charleston Geechees was a very violent prison gang that refused to tolerate others, so I told her I wasn't interested. For a week though I sensed that the Lord wanted me to go there. That unction was so strong that I thought about it all night while lying in bed. I finally said, "Lord, if you're wanting me to go to Lieber then let the job still be open." So I went to Lieber to cut hair for the staff and inmates.

Once there, I went every day to the rec field to lift weights and play handball. It was there that I met this a short little man who was very meek and mild named Walter. When I first met him, I liked him instantly because he had a hunger to learn about the life of Jesus. I talked to him every day about Jesus' miracles and the love Jesus showed others as He walked the shores of Galilee and the land of Israel.

You may have heard of Walter because he was partner to Pee Wee, South Carolina's worst serial killer. At one time Walter was scary like his partner, Pee Wee. Because most inmates rarely talk about their crimes and we don't ask, I didn't know this for months.

As I said, Walter loved to play handball and I loved to talk about my Savior, so as we played daily, I would tell Walter how Jesus loved him and died to redeem him and wanted to save him. He had a hard time believing that Jesus could forgive him, just as I did when I repented in the county jail. But I reminded him daily of a man whom God loved, a man named David who committed murder and adultery, yet was a man after God's own heart. I showed him where the Bible told the story of a prophet named Nathan who told David that God had put away his sin. Both of David's sins carried a death penalty just as Walter's did, but God forgave David after he repented. Walter listened intently as I read the Bible to him.

One day when we met on the rec field Walter seemed quieter than usual. Even though he was a shy, quiet man, I sensed he had something besides handball on his mind. I finally asked him why he was so withdrawn. I'll never forget how he ran to me, put his arms around me and said, "Jimmy, I've been thinking about Jesus and how He loved everybody and forgave them of their crimes. I've seen from what you've read that God can even forgive me, but I don't know what to do to get Him to forgive me. What do I do?" This short little man looked like he wouldn't hurt a flea and he couldn't scare a grandma, but he had participated in brutal murders. Pee Wee's book, *Final Truth: The Autobiography of a Serial Killer*, tells how Walter pulled shoes from the victims to wear. I didn't know any of this at the time. I just knew here was a man I liked to be around because he was humble and wanted to know about Jesus, and now I could see that the Holy Spirit was convicting him of his sins and leading him to repentance. I asked him to bow with me right there on the handball court. I opened my little New Testament Bible and read Romans 10:9 and 13 and Walter accepted Jesus Christ as his personal Savior.

* * *

In 1989, I left Lieber for Wateree River Prison. As we drove up, I noticed right away there were no fences. Yet, as we traveled past the farming area, we could see that it had a 10-foot chain-link fence around its perimeter since it was an A-custody prison.

In late 1990 while I was at Wateree, I asked Dr. Davis if he could help me get transferred to the Palmer Work Release Center in Florence which I considered my home. After a few phone calls to his friends, he told me that the warden of Palmer had agreed to accept me on a new Pilot A program. It meant that I would live at Palmer as an inmate worker but with no privileges. I wasn't eligible for the 32-hour passes the other inmates received. After four years being on staff, I would have 10 years in SCDC, making me eligible for passes. Unless he made parole, this was as good as it gets for someone doing a life sentence, so I was ecstatic over this. The main reason the warden at Palmer wanted me was because Palmer had plans to build a canteen and I was chosen to run it.

Dr. Davis stressed my honesty and Christianity. I had no prior record and at that point, I also had a perfect institutional record. After a few months at Wateree I was told one night in April 1991 that early the next morning I would be inventoried, packed and shipped to Palmer. A few of my friends came around to say goodbye and asked if I could help them get there.

The next morning, I arrived at Palmer. At first, I was assigned to the main building and went to work in the maintenance department. Shortly after that we began to build the canteen. I told the supervisor I was an experienced roofer and he agreed that when he got to the roof, I could put it on. However, he listened to another man who told him he was a roofer and could do the job. The building was small but had a small porch that protruded lower than the roof. That man and his helper put that small porch on but when it ran up to the roof, he didn't know how to tie the two together. The supervisor sent for me and asked could I fix it. I said, "If you'll get those two men off that roof and give me one man to carry the shingles up, I'll have your roof on this afternoon." Once the roof was on, SCDC sent a canteen truck down and I began managing the canteen.

Shortly after I arrived, Palmer got a new warden named Mr. James Sligh. Since I had been elected as the Inmate Advisory Council (IAC) chairman, I met with Mr. Sligh once a month to go over problems and suggestions. At one meeting Mr. Sligh said that the farmers market had been given a field across the street to use in perpetuity and asked if I had any ideas. While I was in prison, I had gotten quite good at handball so I asked Mr. Sligh for permission to build a handball court. I told him I also wanted to build a softball field and picnic tables for our weekend visitors. He gave permission.

As president of the IAC, I was also over the camera project, so on weekends I would sell pictures to the inmates that had been taken of them and their families. I had already generated $300-$400 from the camera project so our account had a decent start. I was able to call around and get the blocks for our court at a discount. Mr. Sligh took me out of the canteen and gave me a two-man crew so I could get started.

I laid out the bases, the pitcher's diamond and began shoveling out the grass so I could have a clay infield. Mr. Sligh put up a memorandum that stated if any inmate was a concrete worker/finisher or block mason to go see me, and if they helped to put up a handball court, they'd be given an extra 32-hour pass. The second day out there my two helpers didn't come back, but in SCDC no inmate tells on another or tells him what to do.

At Palmer, all the inmates were short-timers so they hadn't been in maximum security for six years like I had. I loved to be outside working and to be working alone made it even sweeter, so I wasn't going to say anything. When I finished the ball diamond, I filled a 55-gallon drum with water and rolled it across the diamond to pack the dirt. Then I took a set of post hole diggers and dug holes for the poles to make a backstop. Within two weeks we had a ball field and a handball court.

When the ball field was finished, I called Bro. Carl at Lamb's Chapel to invite them to come out on Sunday afternoon to mingle, minister and play softball with the inmates who hadn't gotten passes. My sons always came so I got to play softball on the same team with them. The church would also have a hot dog roast and feed the inmates. It was a great time in the Lord. And coming out on Tuesday evenings was the ex-mayor of Florence, Mr. C. Cooper Tedder.

I had talked about playing handball with my sons and now they got to see me play, plus I taught them how to play. We had great visits because the Lord had made it all possible.

I also dug out a volleyball court and bought a load of sand for it. I dug out an area and surrounded it with tires that were put halfway in the ground with a jungle gym set and swings a C/O donated so children visiting their dads could have a place to play. With money from the IAC account, I bought lumber and made picnic tables that I placed around the field.

Because there were no shade trees, I bought 20 awnings that I'd rent to our visitors so they had shade. Before long we had 30 awnings that rented for $3 for the day. Mr. Sligh said it wasn't fair that I had to leave my visit to put up awnings, so he said to donate $15 a day to someone to put them up. I decided that since my boys and I could have one up in under five minutes, we could do it. If the occupants left I could re-rent that awning and the $3 was my reward. The Lord blessed me to be able to buy awnings and food by me deciding to do it myself.

CHAPTER 25

I need to explain what I'm about to tell: back in 1985, I didn't have a trial, but instead I had been in the county jail since October 18, 1984. My lawyer convinced me to spare everybody the pain of a difficult trial by pleading guilty, so I did. After being sent to prison, I studied cases similar to mine in the law library. I found many discrepancies. I filed for a Post-Conviction Relief Hearing.

The State Supreme Court granted my hearing, so in March 1988, I went to my hearing, and my case was overturned and my conviction set aside. On the advice of my appellant lawyer, I didn't file a Motion for a Speedy Trial, and I remained in prison for the next four years. The State had appointed an ambulance-chaser lawyer named Tim A. to represent me. We met a few times between 1985 and 1992 to arrange with the Solicitor's Office for me to plea to a lesser charge of manslaughter. But with the opposition I had, we never reached that. Mr. A. tried to defend me but he wasn't a criminal lawyer, and this was his first case.

On January 10, 1992, I was taken from Palmer to the county jail in Dillon to start my trial the following week. On Monday morning Mr. A. came to the back of the courtroom to tell me the State had a plea bargain agreement for me. He said, "If you'll plead guilty to manslaughter and accept 30 years max and then plead guilty to 'assault and battery with intent to kill'" for the man I shot at the gas station, they'd give me the max of 20 years but would run them consecutively for 50 years. I turned it down because at the time I was in for only six years and 50 years looked impossible to do.

The State brought the lead prosecutor from Bennettsville to join with the deputy solicitor from Dillon to make sure all their I's were dotted and all their T's were crossed so they could put me away for life. I feel the devil doesn't want me out of prison because I have a lot to share with the youth in churches, schools or jails that would deter them from going to prison.

Even the judge was handpicked because he had been a great law student and wouldn't allow them to make any mistakes that could get me back in court. He knew there was a conflict of interest with him because when he was a lawyer I went to his office and he loaned me $50 which I failed to return. He never forgot that and was prejudiced against me. He was a hometown boy who was raised with my victim. So here sat a judge who was prejudiced against me, along with two solicitors who had promised the victim's family that they would get me life, and here I sat with an ambulance chaser for a lawyer (no disrespect meant, please). I didn't have a chance at a fair trial.

My lawyer never mentioned my mental condition at the time. As a matter of fact, he couldn't even mention that I had been in prison for six years already and my case had been overturned. We had subpoenaed Mr. Bruton to tell how I may have saved his life during the Kirkland riot but he couldn't testify. Nobody could help me. My trial lasted for three days and a jury found me guilty of murder and I was sent back to Palmer with a life sentence. I was given my jail and prison time so my six years counted. If I had taken that plea deal, I would've maxed it out two years ago and been free to work for the Lord without these chains, but I believe the Lord was even in that decision. Why? Only He knows.

For an inmate, I became powerful at Palmer and one of the captains resented me and began to persecute me, eventually having me shipped. An incident occurred since then and I need for God to get the glory. I met a man named Robert.

When I was being shipped and the belly chains and ankle bracelets were put on me, I was so hurt. On the ride to the Florence County Jail, I started praying and asking the Lord, "Why?" I told Him that I knew He was in control of my life but how could He let that captain ship me out. I was comfortable at Palmer. I had prestige, I had a job I loved and my family was only a few miles away. They visited me on Saturdays and Sundays and we talked all the time. I could go with the inmates to movies. I'd call my family and they'd come and we'd sit together. So, I was hurt and confused. But God knows all things.

If He's called you to work for Him, it doesn't matter how comfortable you are because when or where He needs you, that what's important. From the very beginning when I finally surrendered, God was using me for His purposes in prison. He didn't owe me an explanation, but I can look back and see what He was doing.

The hottest news at that time was about a man

from Florence who stabbed an old man and his wife to death and stole their car. The suspect's name was Robert and he had been arrested and was in the Florence County Jail. The State was seeking the death penalty. When I arrived at the Florence County Jail, I was placed in a bloc downstairs where there were five small cells. When the C/O left and locked the main door behind him, a man came from the last cell to my cell and started talking to me. He asked what I was going to court for so I told him how I had been sentenced to life in prison for murder, had already served for six and a half years and was now being shipped from Palmer. He said, "Have you heard about the double homicide case involving a man and woman on TV news lately?"

I answered, "Yes, it's hot news."

He said, "That's my work." And he began to tell me all about it, how he did it and why.

I told him "Man, you need to be careful who you tell all that to." I then began to talk to him about Christ. I told him about my conversion, my family, and he asked me to pray for him. I prayed for him and I asked God to please save him somewhere in his life.

The next morning, I was sent to the R&E Center at Lieber to be reassigned to an institution, but Robert was still in my mind so I continued to pray for him. A few days later I was sent to an A-custody prison in Columbia, so I called my dear friend, Dr. Davis, to tell him where I was.

During our conversation, I told him that I had been sent to the Florence County Jail and I had met the man who killed the old man and woman, that he had told me how and why he did it. Dr. Davis said, "Jimmy, you need to tell someone about that because it's just the right thing to do." I remember telling him that I didn't want to do that because the State had plenty of evidence on him already, and I didn't want to get involved so we dropped it.

A few days later I was told to go to the conference room because two police investigators from Florence wanted to talk to me. I was escorted in and asked to sit down. They had a picture of Robert and asked had I ever seen him. I told them, "Yes, I met him at the county jail."

They said, "If we have to call on you to testify what would you want?"

I said, "What do you mean? What would I want?"

He said, "Would a guarantee of making parole the first time up be something you'd be interested in?"

I told them if I were to testify it would be because it was my decision and not because of any guarantees or special treatments. But I wasn't going to put a man on death row for any reason.

They said, "But we can subpoena you and make you testify."

I said, "But you know what, my memory gets worse every year so I may forget everything." They picked up their tape recorder and left. I heard later from Dr. Davis that the State found Robert guilty of premeditated murder with aggravated circumstances and placed him on South Carolina's death row. So, I started praying for his soul. I wanted him to repent and find peace.

Then in 1997, when I was at Lee County Prison, I was told to go to the visiting room because my lawyers wanted to see me. I told our unit Lt. that I didn't have a lawyer. He said, "There's two lawyers up there waiting to see you so go on up there."

I said, "But I don't have a lawyer or a case in court so could you please call up there and see if it's me they want or is someone making a mistake."

He called and was told to send me on up. I was sent

to a conference room in the visiting area where I was met by two nicely dressed, beautiful women who were from the appellate court and assigned to Robert's case. They were hunting evidence to use to try to overturn Robert's case. They questioned me about what Robert had said to me. I told them everything and I told them about the two South Carolina agents visiting me and what I had told them. I told them to please leave me out of it because I didn't want to do any harm to anyone again, and I certainly didn't want to be partly responsible for helping to execute a man. Again, I felt led to continue to pray for Robert.

Fifteen years have passed (at the time of this writing) since I saw Robert's two lawyers so I forgot about him until I met a man here at Lieber named Bud who had been on death row but had his case overturned and was given a life sentence so I asked Bud about Robert. Bud said Robert still had a few appeals left when he left death row so again, I prayed for Robert. Finally, Bud left our building; for two years I had prayed for Robert.

About two weeks later, I saw a new man in our building and for the next few days I observed how quiet and peaceful he was. I began a conversation with him. He was a tender-hearted soft-spoken gentle man and I sensed by his language and that he didn't cuss, that he acted like someone who was a Christian. I asked him where he was from. He said Florence. I said "I'm from Florence too," so we talked about Florence for 10 or 15 minutes. He never used a single word of profanity which is unusual for prisoners, so I asked him if he knew Christ.

He lit up and began witnessing of his love for Christ. Then he said, "I got saved on death row. I was on death row for 20 years."

I looked at his name tag and all I could say was

"Praise God!"

He said, "What's your name?"

I said, "Robert, I've praying for you for 21 years now."

He asked, "How?"

I said, "Do you remember meeting a man in the county jail who had been at Palmer Work Release Center and was being shipped?"

He softly said, "Are you Jimmy?"

I said, "Yes," and with that I hugged Robert, my brother in and because of Christ.

Thank God that He is a merciful loving and forgiving creator or none of us would be saved. David in the Bible was a murderer but repented, so was Paul the Apostle. I'm so sorry for my crime and I hope one day everyone can forgive me, but I can thank God every day that He sent His Son to die for me and it's Jesus' own blood that washed away all my sins. Praise God!

Because someone had complained about me at the Palmer Work Release Center, I was sent back to the R&E Center. From the R&E Center I was assigned to Stevenson Correctional Institute in Columbia by Mr. Avery who was the classification director. Mr. Avery knew me from Lieber and Palmer. He knew I stood firmly for the Lord and was a hard worker in the I.A.C. to help inmates, so when he saw me being marched into the R&E Center in ankle chains and belly chains, he looked at me and said, "Not you. I expected better from you."

All I said was, "I'm not guilty of anything, Mr. Avery," and was led away to my cell.

The next day he came to my cell and said, "I checked up on you, and you really didn't do anything to be shipped, so you tell me where do you want to go."

I said, "to Columbia." Five days later I was in an A-custody prison in Columbia and, being closer to Bro. David Harmon, he visited me a lot more. My kids and I had gotten close again and, even being in Columbia, they still visited me every two weeks.

CHAPTER 26

In 1996, I received a letter from a lady named Bonnie. She said she had seen my brother Hal and he told her I was in doing life in prison on a murder conviction. She said, "Not Jimmy. If he had said Clifton, I would've believed him, but not Jimmy. He was the good one."

I thought, "Who is this woman? She knows me but I don't remember a Bonnie A." I only knew a Bonnie J. Instantly, it hit me. This is my Bonnie. In her letter, she said her husband Harold had recently died. She asked me to write her, so I wasted no time writing back. She asked me to call her and gave me her number. We became instant friends again so she started coming to visit me.

We needed each other just as we did when we were kids and so finally, after all the years of knowing we loved each other, we got married. We snuck into the men's bathroom which is outside of S.C.I. and consummated our marriage.

Bonnie is somewhat like me when it comes to

remembering things. She tells me I have the memory of an elephant, and I always say mine is better. She asked me if had I ever seen or heard from my daughter Jennifer in North Carolina and I said no. I said I had tried a few times to get people to help me find her now that she's over 18 and can make her own choices. She said, "I'll help you."

But before she could, David Beasley, who was the governor of South Carolina, hired a man from Texas named Michael Moore to be the commissioner over the prisons. His first act was to have his C/Os come in the middle of the night and pack up and ship inmates with violent crimes back to B-custody. Dr. Davis had helped me get approved as a driver for Campbell Work Release Center and this time I would be eligible for 32- and 74-hour passes with my children picking me up. But I was shipped from Stevenson Correctional Institute to Lee Correctional Institute.

In 1997, while I was at Lee, Bonnie and I visited every week and our love was so strong, I couldn't wait to see her again. We had gotten to know all the C/Os by name and we also became friends with other inmates and their wives who visited each week. I was at Lee for only a year because the director over SCDC at the time designated that Lee Prison would be a regional medical facility for 24-hour medical-needs inmates. Unless you had a medical hold, you would be shipped to another institution. Bonnie and I prayed asking the Lord to let us stay as we grew to love our Christian friends and enjoyed the life we had.

But God is in control and His will comes before ours, so even though Bonnie and I had prayed and even talked to the warden about my staying there, I was eventually shipped back to Lieber.

I arrived at Lieber on February 5, 1998. When you transfer from one prison to another, they screen you in many ways. One is you have to go to Medical for a physical and two is you go to the education department for a TABK test to see if you need to be educated. After I had been at Lieber for two days I was sent to Medical that morning for my physical. A nurse had taken all the vitals and sent me to the back of the infirmary for blood work. I sat in the hallway with other inmates and a C/O at a desk nearby. In that area of Medical there are six to eight rooms with hospital beds for inmates who are in need of full medical service for 24 hours a day.

I missed Bonnie, I missed my friends and I missed Lee Prison because it was close to my home in Florence. I even questioned the Lord and asked Him why couldn't He let me stay at Lee Prison where I was comfortable.

As I sat there, I was meditating on my Bible reading that morning. I had read where Paul had been warned by other Christians to not travel to Jerusalem for there were Pharisees who wanted to kill him. Paul wasn't concerned for his life because he felt God wanted him to witness for Jesus. As I thought on Paul's words, I remembered the last night's prayer and my words of surrender to God's will.

It had been years since I had heard anything about Walter, Pee Wee's partner (Pee Wee - the worst serial killer South Carolina ever had.) But an orderly wheeled a little grey-haired man directly in front of me and told the C/O to watch him while he went back to clean his room and change his sheets.

At first, I paid no attention, but God is so wonderful. I began to look at this little old terribly sick man sitting in front of me when a nurse came out and asked, "Walter, are you okay?" I still didn't catch on to what God was doing, but I kept hearing her say "Walter." I knew only one man named Walter so as I started looking at him, his head was bent low but he raised up and looked at me. I said, "Are you Walter N.?"

He said, "Yes, who are you?"

I said, "Walter, it's me, Jimmy, Jimmy Windham."

Oh, listen people, it was so sweet because I saw a loving Savior at work. That little broken down man grabbed my hand and he said in desperate-sounding words, "Jimmy, tell me again, does Jesus still love me and forgive me?"

I got down on my knees beside him and I held him in my arms with everyone watching and I told him, "Walter, yes Jesus loves you and has forgiven you." Walter cried and held on to me as I sang Amazing Grace in his ear.

The next day Walter died. I knew then why God had sent me back to Lieber so I stopped questioning the Lord. Jesus said once, "If you seek to save your life, you'll lose it but if you lose your life for My sake, you'll find it."

Over the years in here I've learned what that means. I'm sure Paul the apostle knew well what Jesus meant by those words for I see in Him my life for Christ. God takes someone He has chosen and places them wherever He wills because the Kingdom of God comes first. I've learned, sometimes the hard way, that my will doesn't come first with God.

Notice Paul said in Romans 8, "And we know that for those who love God all things work together for good, for those who are called according to his purpose." People love to quote that, but finish that verse, because in it lies the true meaning of the good for us mentioned, for it said "for those who are called according to His [God's] purpose." Not my will, not your will, but God's will. When you've been chosen for a mission in your life, then you'll always see that later on it was for your good.

At Lieber, I was put back in Stono Dorm into a three-man room sleeping on the floor half under the other two prisoner's beds with no locker for my personal belongings. And to make it worse, both my roommates were black which for me wasn't a problem, but for them it was - me being white. One of them even told me the first day I was moved in there that he hated white men and didn't want me to speak or talk to him. I stayed an agonizing two months in that room; but I would share my food at times with the one who began to like me. I had a TV and I would always ask them what they would like to watch when two movies were on different channels. At the end of my two months I finally got to move into a two-man room with an old friend of mine named John. John has since passed on, but before he died, he had converted to Christ.

The day I moved I was making my last load from the three-man room when the black man who had told me he hated white men stopped me at the door. He said, "Jimmy, give me a minute" and closed the door. He said, "When you first moved into this room, I told you of my hate for white people, but I watched your life and I listened to your talk and I honestly say that as a Christian man you not only talked the talk but you've walked the walk, and I have nothing but respect for you." He took my hand and pulled me to him and hugged my neck.

CHAPTER 27

I still had much pain over not knowing my daughter, Jennifer, and I had given Bonnie information on how I thought I could find my daughter. On our visit in December 1998 Bonnie dropped a telephone number on our table, slid it over to me and simply said, "Call your daughter."

On December 21, 1998, I called her number. The operator said, "You have a collect call from Jimmy Windham."

All the fears and anxiety ended when I heard my daughter say, "Daddy, is this really you?"

I said, "Yes."

She said, "I've prayed for this moment."

I said, "Me, too. I'm sorry I'm in prison so I can't come see you."

She said, "Let me just hear your voice. We'll get to the rest later." We talked our 15 minutes.

I gave her my address and asked, "Do you think you'll ever want to come see me?"

And she said something that thrilled me to my soul. She said, "I'll pray about it." To me that meant she loved the Lord and also prayed about things in her life; and that also meant I would see her because I knew God didn't get all of this started to end in only a phone call.

About five months later I walked into the visiting room at Lieber with my Ray-Bans on. She told me later that she had told her friend Crystal, who accompanied her, "That's my daddy. Only he and I would walk into a room wearing shades."

She waved at me and I went over to our table where she was standing. I walked up and took her into my arms and the angels started singing. I looked into her big blue eyes that could only be mine because Alice had green eyes. I could've picked her out of a crowd because all my children look like me and look alike. She and my angel Shelley could pass for twins: same height, same build, same button nose, same smile and same eyes. From that day on we lived and breathed each other. We got so infatuated with each other that we neglected those around us and it began to cause problems. She told a friend that even a pair of socks reminded her of me. It was as if we couldn't get enough after all the years of missing each other.

I neglected Bonnie so much that she stopped coming to visit me and because of my neglect and other problems, we got a divorce.

Jennifer told me if I could get transferred to Evans C.I. which is in Bennettsville and a few miles from the North Carolina line she could come visit me more, so I put in for a hardship transfer to be closer to home; and three months later I was at Evans. Jennifer began to visit me every two weeks and we ran up steep phone bills. It got so bad that her husband had to put his foot down because we were out of control. I blame it all now on all the emptiness, yearning and lost love and time we had missed out on for 33 years.

We finally got used to each other and she left so she could take care of her family. I involved myself in my job. I was hired as a board runner making very intricate telecommunication cables for the U.S. Government. It was a highly-skilled job so each employee was paid minimum wage.

Though I had gotten my GED in 1998, I also had enrolled in some college courses to receive my Associate of Arts in Theology. But South Carolina took our Pell grants because we were prisoners. I enrolled in two-year correspondence college-level courses from Ambassador College in Edmond, Oklahoma, and received a degree. Always wanting to better myself I also went back to an official high school here at Lieber and graduated with my high school diploma. After two years in Prison Industries I was made lead man over a section. For an inmate in prison that was as good as it gets.

Though we make minimum wages, South Carolina found a way to take 55% of our earnings for their expenses (room and board, victim witness fund, etc.). Plus, we pay state and federal taxes and into a long-term savings account that we can only use once we get out of prison. I have over $4,000 in that account and SCDC draws the interest on it. I worked on that job for over nine years.

SCDC changed their classification again in 2010 stating that any inmate with a life sentence who has had a write-up (including minor write-ups) within 10 years would be shipped from all level 2 institutions back to a level 3.

In 2001, I received a minor write-up for abuse of privileges. SCDC has a two-hug or two-kiss limit in the visiting room. Without thinking I kissed and hugged Jennifer once when I walked into the visiting room and when visits were over, we stood up at our table and hugged, and when I walked her to the desk to say goodbye we hugged and kissed. I know it's ridiculous but a rule is a rule so I was written up. Now I've been back at Lieber for 2½ years.

I know God is in control so I look at it as though He's leading me. I notice that the institution has more of a hunger for the Lord which allows me to have a strong witness for the Lord.

CHAPTER 28

I had begun to write short articles that I would send to various ministries and ask them to attach my tract-like story to their mailings going out to inmates. Kenneth Copeland, Creflo Dollar and a few I saw on TV sent me word that they couldn't do that even though it was a good article. They said if they did it for me, they'd have to do it for everyone.

One article I had written was about Abraham offering up Isaac being similar to God offering up Christ. I called it *A Blood Covenant*. I sent a copy to Bro. Phillip Hayes from Pleasant Hill, Tennessee. Someone gave me one of his magazines that had his address in it. He wrote me to tell me how it blessed him and asked if he could publish it in his next magazine. Of course, I said yes, because this was my first time to be used of the Lord in such a great way. At the end of it he wrote "Bro. Windham is in prison in South Carolina" and gave my name, number and address. Bro. Hayes and I became friends and he even drove down to Columbia to see me. He had a strong witness and God led him to the mission field with his wife to do a great work. Somehow, we lost contact, but God used him to put *A Blood Covenant* in his magazine with my address.

I got a few letters from around the States and God sent me a guardian angel in one who had read my article. A sweet little old grandmother named Miss Edna Miller from Barbeau, Michigan, began to write to me. We wrote every week and shared our lives. She told me about her deceased husband named John and that because they lived near one of Michigan's lakes, they fished a lot.

She sent me pictures of her, her children, and her grandchildren. She was a sweet, wonderful grandmother and she told me because my Granny died when I was in prison that she adopted me and would be my Granny. So, to me she was family, and I soon loved her as if she *were* my Granny. She went on to be with the Lord a few years ago, but while she was here, she kept me encouraged in the Lord and would send me books. I still have a Bible dictionary she bought for me. I never met Grandmother Miller in person but I know soon I'll get to meet her and John together. Before she went to sleep in the Lord, she asked her precious daughter Marilyn and her husband, Sonny Veit, to watch over me and we, too, became close and like family.

Bro. Sonny sends me books that he knows will uplift and strengthen me, and he was very instrumental of the Lord to encourage me to continue writing when I thought I couldn't because I was digging up too much pain. He prayed with me and the Holy Spirit began to help me to write. Bro. Sonny drove down once to visit me, and his face shone with the light of God that is within him. I thank God for him and Sister Marilyn.

They, along with Dr. Davis and my kids, were my strength when the South Carolina Parole Board turned me down. I had made plans with Brother Sonny to go to Dr. Davis' church to speak on the pitfalls of drugs and alcohol and the forgiveness of sin when we give our lives to Christ; but when I was rejected, I emptied my pain that day onto Brother Sonny and Sister Marilyn's shoulders. That's when we decided that if I can't be set free to go do a work for the Lord, I can write it all down and send it out to prisons, churches and book stores so God can still be glorified by my life.

In 2005, I wrote another article that I entitled *The Love of Jehovah, the God and Father of our Lord Jesus Christ*. In it I stated I had been in prison at that time, for 21 years, and there hasn't been one day that I haven't witnessed to someone the Lord has caused to cross my path. That still holds true today. My roommate, Morris, is also a follower of the Law of God and the faith of Jesus Christ and is also enrolled in Ambassador College. Morris says that I'm a walking Bible, but I've studied the scriptures these past 34 years to hide His Word in my heart so I can be pleasing to God.

I've gotten close to a precious brother in the Lord in McMinnville, Tennessee, named Alfred King. He's one of the pastors of a church there who also puts out a monthly magazine entitled the *Testimony of Truth*. Bro. Al King read the original manuscript of my book and in his next letter to me he said, "God was very patient and merciful to you."

I thought about his words and to me it sounded like he meant that God was ready to cut me off at any minute before my conversion and imprisonment. I thought it meant that I was lucky I made it in.

I responded to him because I've come to see that

God is and always was in total control of a called and chosen person's life. I said "Bro. Al, when Stephen was being stoned to death as a martyr for his outstanding love for Jesus that, as harsh as it seems, it was God's perfect will for Stephen's life. But at the same time there was another chosen man in God's perfect will who held their coats as Stephen was stoned named Saul of Tarsus. God allowed circumstances of Paul's life to make him into the person he would become and it was those circumstances that qualified him for the mission he would accomplish for his Savior. So, I believe that Paul became what God made him to be." After I wrote him and asked what he meant, he wrote back and I knew he didn't mean it the way I took it, and was actually praising God for His longsuffering and endless mercy.

I always felt I wanted to do a work for the Lord. I've seen many preachers come in here and preach to us. Some are so soft and afraid to step on toes that it's like sugar drips from their lips, while others scream at us that unless we come down and as they hold our hands and repeat a prayer, we're lost souls forever.

I believe that they all go back to their comfortable churches and tell their congregation about numbers. Tonight, we had 25 inmates who came forward, etc. But how many would come live in here for the rest of their lives for Christ for even one? I dare to say none! But Paul had to.

CHAPTER 29

On January 10, 2015, I had to be rushed by ambulance to Trident Medical Center at Charleston, South Carolina, because I had severe blockage in three arteries that went into my heart. They performed a triple by-pass open-heart surgery. Before my surgery, the doctor, Dr. Roberts, came into my hospital room to see if I was prepared psychologically for what I was facing. He sat beside me and said, "Mr. Windham, I don't want you to worry over what is about to happen because I've performed a thousand of these operations, and I've never lost anyone, so I feel confident that I won't lose you. Do you have any questions?"

I asked him how long would it take to operate on me?

He said, "You'll be out of your room for possibly seven or more hours. I'll give you something to help you relax and I'll come by and check on you as soon as you're awake."

I asked him if he believed in Jesus Christ. He

responded with a "Yes, I do."

I asked if he would pray with me. He said, "yes" and bowed his head. He silently prayed as he held my hand. When he left, I still was experiencing the anxiety I had felt since being rushed to the hospital in an ambulance three days earlier.

I knew this was life or death. I knew I could die when my heart was taken out of my chest. I still had my eyes closed, so I prayed, "Father, when I first came to prison 34 years ago, the cry of my heart was for you to take care of my children and keep them safe. Father, you've blessed them and kept them, so all I can do is thank you, for they really don't need me. If you take me, they'll miss me for a while, but they'll be okay, so if you leave me here, don't leave me here for them. They don't need me. But leave me for your kingdom."

While the C/O who was guarding me took off the ankle chains that shackled me to the bed, I opened my eyes and told the nurses "I thought you were going to give me something to help me relax." It seemed I had just closed my eyes, but it was actually seven or more hours later. I was out of surgery and I realized, "I'm alive! I'm alive!"

Now I'm being honest and God must have a sense of humor, for I do. I looked down and I was chained by my ankle to the bed. I looked to my left where a C/O was sitting in a chair with a .38 pistol. I looked to my right where the other C/O sat in a chair asleep with a newspaper on her lap. I heard myself say "Or am I." I stayed there for two more days, and if I could've, I would've done the rest of my time in the hospital, for compared to SCDC prison food, the food at the hospital was gourmet. Unfortunately for me, I was discharged to the infirmary (prison hospital) at Kirkland for eight days.

When I left Kirkland, I was sent back to my same room at Lieber with Ralph as my roommate. I was in a wheelchair for a month, but I determined that I wouldn't let my body stop me from regaining my health.

After a month, I forced myself to get up, and once a day I would go to the small fenced-in rec field outside our back door and walk for 15 minutes for a week. The next week I was up to 30 minutes a day. The third week for 45 minutes and I walked vigorously. When I was up to an hour of vigorous walking, my health was better.

I was on seven pills in the morning and I had to take four at night. When they take your heart out, you lose all your strength for all your organs are so weak, so I was taking medicine for diabetes, high blood pressure and anything else they used to keep me alive. After the first two months out of the infirmary, I was taken off the insulin shots and put onto the pill. I took 1000 mg of Metformin twice a day and my A1C was 14.9.

A year after I left the hospital, I signed a refusal to take all the medicines except the Metformin for I was diagnosed as a Type 2 diabetic. Today, 3 ½ years later, I only take 500 mg of Metformin twice a day. I've lost over 50 pounds because I still walk vigorously for an hour daily. I was at Medical in April to have blood work so I could be checked again and the nurse practitioner said, "Mr. Windham, whatever you're doing, keep it up for your A1C is 6.7 and when you come back in six months to have it checked again, if it is under six, which it looks as though it will be, I'm taking you off of the medication we have you on." I know the dieting and exercise may not cure all diseases in everybody. I give God the praise for it did in me.

Now back to the request I made of my Father that day as I lay flat on my back in Trident Medical Center. I said, "If you leave me here, leave me here for You, for Your kingdom."

The medical department moved my roommate Ralph and me to the Character Dorm since it was closer to Medical and I guess they expected me to be a patient for a long time, even though I thought differently. I was moved on March 2, 2015, into cell #8. Cell #8 was my old cell when I first was at Lieber in the late 80's, 28 years earlier. Eight in the Bible means New Beginnings and it was very true for me.

So, as I said, when I started this last chapter of this book, around September of 2015, I was sent an order to report to Medical for tests concerning my health. I was placed in the holding cell along with about 10 or 15 other men who came to Medical. I was talking to a man I had known for many years, and he asked me how I was getting along, for he knew of my latest near-death experience. I was witnessing of God's mercy and grace on me and my love for Jesus, my Savior. A man sitting on the bench near me asked a question about my faith in God and when he did, as I looked into his eyes, I saw he wasn't being mean, but was being inquisitive about my faith.

He asked me, "How do you know the faith you have in God is real and not just religious?"

I started to describe my faith in Jesus as my Lord and my loving Savior. But as I started, his name was called by the C/O to see the medical staff, so he was gone. I didn't see him again for two months, but I never forgot how much I wanted to tell him about my faith and I felt led to pray for him.

When I saw him the next time, he was on the serving line in the chow hall and was wearing a Muslim *kufi*. He came out and I approached him. We introduced ourselves and he told me his name was Michael. He asked if I could help him get an interview to move to Stono Character-Based Dorm, so I set out to do just that, for I had been elected as a mentor in Stono. In the dorm I had left to move to Stono before my surgery I was a Peer Leader, a Program Coordinator, and a Facilitator of Character Principles, so the Program Coordinators in Stono sent Mike an O.T.R. to come for an interview because they knew me and knew I wouldn't tell them that Mike was a good man if he wasn't.

It took about two months for a bed to open up on Stono Dorm before Mike could move in. I was still praying for him and asking God to move him near me, for I was burdened to tell him about the precious Lord Jesus and knew He also loved Michael. They moved him to the other side of my dorm, so I still couldn't talk with him, for at that time, the two sides couldn't mix together. But when God puts someone on your heart, it's because He wants to use us as a vessel of honor for their benefit. Just be faithful and humble.

Now here's how the Lord moved. Mike was moved to my side of the dorm because of a run-in with another man. But if you knew Mike, you'd know it wasn't his nature to get into a fuss with anyone. I know that the other man was used by God to get him near me. Mike moved into a cell near me and we became instant friends. For the next year I methodically and meticulously gently led him to Christ.

Then Mike became deathly sick. He looked pale and green. He had so much poison in his system from his swollen gall bladder that it was poisoning his whole body. Anything he ate, he would throw back up. I would go sit with him and pray for him. The only food he could hold down was what I prayed over in

Jesus' name. SCDC is cold and uncaring and Medical almost let him die, but I refused to let him die for he is my friend and I love Mike, so I fasted, giving him my food. I told him every day about Jesus' miracles, and Mike's faith in Christ grew. Like me, he began to walk for health. He began to eat vegetables and color came back into his face.

One morning as I sat at the table in my room, Mike knocked at the door. I ushered him in with a wave. Mike and I shared coffee with each other if either of us had some. This day he had a serious look on his face, and he said, "Jimmy Windham, I want to receive Jesus Christ as my personal Savior."

I said, "Praise God, Mike! Come kneel with me beside my bed where I pray for you every night."

Mike knelt down and confessed himself a sinner and asked Jesus to come into his heart. Man, did that upset the devil, for then Mike went to a Muslim meeting and told them he wasn't coming to their services anymore for he had accepted Christ and was a Christian now. Hell broke out for both of us. The Muslims had a hit out on us both, so we were very cautious wherever we went from then on.

Late 2016, my sister told me that my elderly mom said if I was in a prison closer to her, she'd try to come visit me one more time before she died. Mom was 92 years old at that time. We would write each other and I would talk to her if I could, but it had been 15 years since I had seen my mom, because SCDC had moved me to a prison nearly 200 miles away.

As I mentioned earlier, they had changed their classification system and anyone with a life sentence could not be moved until they did 10 years with no write-ups. I was in a level two institution; Lieber and Lee are level three. So, in January of 2017, at my annual review, I put in for a hardship transfer to go to

Lee Institution, and on April 17th I was transferred to Lee. Though I still haven't seen my mom, I'm comforted knowing that I'm finally close to her and my home.

The parting between Mike and me was painful and tearful. My heart ached for having to leave my friend behind. Mike had given me his mom's address and phone number and address so I could write or call her to check on Mike. Mike also said he planned to put in for a hardship transfer at his next annual review to be near his mom.

I didn't write to his mom but I continued praying for him. I felt led to send a letter to Bro. Al King who is the editor of a monthly magazine called, *The Testimony of Truth,* and I asked him if he would forward it to Mike. SCDC doesn't allow its inmates to write to each other, but it was God's will for me to encourage Mike in the Lord, so Bro. Al agreed to forward it to him.

I didn't hear from Mike until I called his mom about six months later. She said she had a letter there from him and would send it to me. A week later I received a form from our mail room saying I had gotten a contraband letter from an inmate and SCDC doesn't – Blah, Blah, Blah – and it was returned to sender, so I called his mom and she read it to me over the phone. He sounded okay.

Two weeks after I left Lieber and arrived at Lee, I hired on at Prison Industries on the West Yard. The West Yard is separated from the East Yard by fences and buildings, but both yards are part of Lee Prison. Both yards have three dorms on them. The West Yard houses the mental health patients, and the most violent inmates live in Dorms #3 and #5. Unless you've been disciplinary-free for at least a year, you can't live in a dorm on the East Yard. When I first came to Lee, I was placed on the West Yard in the mental health dorm because the East Yard didn't have a bed available.

I held a Bible study each night in a day room of the dorm. I had worked in the West Yard for about six months, when the warden toured the dorm I lived in. I had known the warden years earlier at another institution. He was glad to see me but asked why I was in dorm #1. I said I was told there wasn't a bed yet in the Character Dorm on the East Yard. He took my number and a week later I was transferred to the East Yard where I was placed in the Character Building.

I worked in the East Yard as a machine operator making all the uniforms that SCDC inmates wear. I really hated to leave though, for six men gave their lives to the Lord; two of those men have died since.

I'd been in East Yard Prison Industries for seven months when our clerk at work asked if I knew a man named Puerto Rico. I didn't know who he was talking about, but I hoped he was talking about Mike who I hadn't heard from in months. Since Mike's family was from Puerto Rico and we called Mike "Rico," I was hoping it was him. When the clerk described him, I knew it was Mike. I asked why he was asking.

He said, "I saw him at the bus terminal and he asked if I knew Jimmy Windham."

So, I said, "Yes, I know him, we worked together."

He said, "Mike has transferred here."

I said, "Man, you just made my day! No, you made my year!"

So, I asked if he would check his computer to see where Mike was placed. Mike and I both left Lieber from the Character Dorm and we both were placed on the most dangerous and violent yard where neither of us belonged. From the day I heard that Mike was here, I tried to get him moved to my dorm so we could be together again. I asked my supervisor for an application so he could get a job in Prison Industries to start the proactive lifestyle again. A friend had come from another institution and he was working at Prison Industries. I asked him to take a note along with an application for employment to Mike, which he did.

Mike replied telling me how dangerous and ungodly the dorm was and that he feared for his life. When I heard that, I was more diligent trying to get him moved. Finally, two weeks later he was told by Classification to report to work. What a reunion we had that day. We talked and laughed all day, but at 4 p.m. when we got off and went to the chow hall, I could tell he was very troubled knowing he had to go back to his dorm.

During the next few days, I took him to our unit counselor and begged her to move him, but she told me there wasn't a single bed open in our dorm, so she couldn't move him out of Dorm #3. Dorm #3 already had a few stabbings, and men had to be medevacked out just prior to Mike's arrival.

Then, for the next day or two I tried to get him moved to Dorm #2 or the East Yard, but Mrs. McCullough, the unit manager, said she didn't have a bed open there either.

When Mike came to work on Thursday morning, he was terrified. He said the gang had surrounded him the night before and told him they were going to kill him as soon as the word came down from their Lieutenant. He had written a letter to his mom telling her goodbye and that he loved her. He asked her to tell his kids goodbye and that he loved them. He made me promise to send it to her if he died.

It nearly broke my heart to see my friend, who I had grown to love as my own family, so terrified. So, we tried with the help of our supervisor, who is also a good Christian man to call the units on our yard to get Mike a bed, but nothing happened. When we got off work and had to part, Mike hugged me as though it was his last time. He looked in my eyes and said, "Jimmy Windham, I love you, Brother." He turned and walked away.

That was on Thursday afternoon and at that time Prison Industries wasn't working on Fridays, so on Thursday night I was on my knees bombarding Heaven asking God to keep him safe over the week-end, for our unit counselor said she'd have a bed for him the next week. Anyone else would've just stopped and waited on that plan, but not me. I've been in here for 34 years and I've seen things go sour at a moment's notice. Besides, in my spirit, I felt danger brewing.

Then on Friday morning at breakfast, I saw Mrs. McCullough and I went to her and asked her again to move Mike. She said she had only one bed open and another inmate was supposed to move into it that day, so she couldn't move him. So again, I travailed in prayer for him in the Holy Spirit. I wept as I asked God to keep him safe. I would pray for him and would tell God, as I did when I prayed for him to be saved, "Please, Father, save him. He's my friend."

It means a lot to me to have a true friend because if you notice as you've read this book about my life, you'd see that I didn't trust others and I didn't have many friends. Now I can thank God for Him placing men of character in my life who have shown me what it means to be a friend and to trust myself with their care. I am also a true friend when God gives me a friend. When I would tell God that Mike is my friend, my God knew what I meant and what Mike means to me. When he needed a friend, I was there for him and

I determined I wouldn't fail him now. That's what friends do. So, on Saturday morning when I went to the cafeteria for brunch, SCDC only feeds us twice on Saturday and Sunday, it was around 10:30 a.m. Again, Mrs. McCullough was running the cafeteria. I went to talk to her.

She instantly said, "Mr. Windham, before you ask, let me tell you again that I don't have a bed for your friend, but maybe I can move him next week."

I said, "Mrs. McCullough, the gang in Dorm #3 surrounded Mike on Wednesday night. They told him that they planned to kill him as soon as they got the leader's okay. Mike is scared for his life and gave me a letter to send to his mama if he gets killed, so let me ask you a question, please Ma'am."

She said, "Okay, Ask me."

I said, "How will you feel Monday if I tell you I had to mail that goodbye letter to Mike's mama because they killed Him?"

She said, "Will you go on the West Yard and help him move?"

I suspect she didn't think I'd go to that dangerous side. I instantly said, "Yes, Ma'am, I'll go."

She got on her radio and called the Dorm #3 B-side C/O and said, "Pack Michael up. Someone is on the way to help him move."

When I got over there, I knew the Lord was with me for three men came up to me in a rush and asked what I was doing over there. I said, "I'm on a mission from my God to deliver a friend of mine from the lion's den."

They looked at each other, then burst into laughter and walked off. Four or five inmates kept coming to the door that was locked and stared at me. I saw men whose faces were filled with hatred, but the C/O wouldn't open their door and Mike walked out pushing the yellow buggy with his property in it. He hugged me and said, "When the C/O came to my cell and told me to pack up, I said 'Jimmy!'"

I helped him get to Dorm #2 and when we stopped at Mrs. McCullough's office, she said, "I moved you on a Saturday only because your friend told me about your letter. I'm a mother, so it touched my heart."

A couple of signs that it was my God answering prayer is: it wasn't logical for her to move him on a Saturday for they planned to move him on Monday, and the inmate who was assigned to that room never showed up on Friday. Another reason that I know God answered my prayers and totally led me was because on Sunday evening, the next day after I moved Mike, Lee County Prison had the worst riot on record.

On April 25, 2018, 27 men or more on the West Yard in Dorm #3 were in a gang war and seven of 27 were murdered and 20 more who were fighting for their lives had to be rushed out in ambulances and helicopters to neighboring hospitals because they were bleeding to death from all the knife wounds they had received in that battle. Lee Prison went on lock down for 29 days. Some of the very ones who threatened to kill Mike were in that battle and possibly were killed. Mike was safe and locked in.

When Mike walked into Prison Industries that morning, after we were let out 29 days later, he rushed past those asking him questions and walked up to me, and what a bear hug he gave me. Then he looked into my eyes and said, "You saved my life."

I bowed my head and said, "No, it wasn't me, it was my God because He loves you."

Now I'm happy to report that our unit counselor told me yesterday that next week she was having Mike moved to my dorm. So, one year and 1 ½ months after leaving Mike at Lieber, my friend and I are back together talking, laughing, and praising God. Only God could have worked all of this out, I'm so happy today in the Lord for He let me live and win Mike to Him. If I had died, nobody would be reading this book today about Mike and his miracle. It all came by our loving Savior, so I hope you've enjoyed my life story and I hope it has touched your life and that it leads you to Jesus.

CHAPTER 30

Until recently I hadn't experienced death in my immediate family, but Hal died, then Clifton died, then my dad died. Knowing God's Word, I know that soon I'll see them again; so even though I mourned their deaths it made it so much easier to let them go.

My precious little 92-year-old mom is still alive and I thank God for her every day. One of her prayers is to see her only son walk out of prison. She's been such a blessing to me since I walked into prison; may God bless and keep you, Mama. I love you! Also, Carolyn is still alive. She and her husband Eddy Davis still live in Utah. May God bless you, Carolyn and Eddy. Jesus is coming and we'll all live forever on God's new earth under the reign of our King Jesus. Keep the faith. And, Carolyn, I'm sorry I let go. Also, a few months ago Bonnie and I started writing again. Pray for us. I don't see or hear from my family like I would like, but I know God has kept His word to me to bless my seed and keep them safe and blessed.

Jennifer, her husband Jeff, and their two children

live in North Carolina. Jennifer operates her own beauty salon; Shelly is in sales and has worked for the same business for over ten years. My son Jimmy works as a maintenance man for the railroad, and my son Billy has a Bachelor of Science degree in computers. My baby boy, little David, is the manager of the Verizon Wireless Store in Florence, and David is a deacon in the church he attends. All of my kids are married and raising their children, so I'm proud of them and thankful to God for helping them learn to cope with life.

So, now that you know that I've been incarcerated nearly one-half of my life you know that I know this system well. If you're in prison and you don't know the Lord as your Savior, Redeemer, and Mediator between God and you, now would be a good time to ask Him to come into your life. But, don't think you can go on doing the things prisoners do. I see the same crowd go forward in every service I've been to and say the same watered-down repetitious prayer someone quotes to them and they repent. A scripture says, "Be not deceived; God is not mocked: for whatsoever a man soweth, that shall he also reap. For he that soweth to his flesh shall of the flesh reap corruption; but he that soweth to the Spirit shall of the Spirit reap life everlasting." And "For Godly sorrow worketh repentance to salvation." So, you must come to God and repent with your whole heart.

Remember how wicked Nineveh was? God told Jonah to go tell them to repent. You know the story and how Jonah ran from God but finally went and told them to repent or God would destroy their city. They repented! They fasted and prayed for three days, and God heard their prayer. They meant business and they believed God's messenger.

Maybe this book is your "messenger" and I'm

asking you to get alone with God in sincere prayer and repent. Do you want to live forever? Well, you can if you'll repent and turn to God. You can't continue in your sins if you repent. You can't use the Grace of God so you can go on in your sins. I see inmates all the time who call themselves born again, some even sing in the choirs, but they still indulge in homosexual acts. They still use drugs and they still get mad and cuss or fight. God will set you free from those things if you repent.

Maybe you're not in prison, maybe you're on the street and running in gangs and you've read this book. You don't want to throw your life away by coming to prison. God has a better life for you and He'll deliver you from any problem, large or small, if you'll just turn to Him. Please listen to someone who knows what it is to lose everything.

In the 34 years that I've lived in maximum-security prison, I lost everything I hold dear, but from day one I was used by God's Holy Spirit to begin to witness for Him and I've lived it. I haven't fallen away from my calling in all these years, so I believe that just as Paul was in God's perfect will even before he knew Jesus, so was I!

God may use some preachers to come in to preach to us and chaplains to feed the young converts, but God has a living witness who has suffered the hardship of prison for over 34 years living right here among serial killers like Walter. You may not believe this but you need Jesus just as Walter did. Walter was just like the thief on the cross who asked Jesus to remember him. We were all born in sin and unless we repent and accept Jesus into our lives as our personal savior, we aren't any better off than a serial killer in God's eyes.

The wages of sin, any sin, is death, and if we don't

accept the only sacrifice God made available for our forgiveness which is the death and blood of His only begotten Son, we won't have eternal life. My prayer is whoever reads this book can find a way to God like I did 34 years ago.

As we look around us, we see that time is getting short for all the things written in the Bible are surely coming to pass, so I urge you to find your way to the cross of Calvary where Jesus died for you. Because as I told Walter over 12 years ago, yes, Jesus loves you and will forgive all your sins.

Turn to the Savior. He died for you so your sins could be washed away by His precious blood. Oh, what a wonderful Savior He is! I couldn't have done this long sentence in prison if He hadn't been with me. Once you turn to Him, He promises to never leave you or forsake you. But you must act. He won't *make* you serve Him.

Living around violent confrontations every day for the past 34 years, I don't have even one act of violence on my record. God changed my stony heart into a heart of flesh and within that heart He put His Holy Spirit. When I would weep many nights from loneliness on my bed, He put friends and family around me to give my life purpose; people who love God like Dr. Thad Davis and his precious wife Jeanette; a man like Bro. David Harmon; and Bro. Sonny and Sister Marilyn Veit; and my children. I'd get a card or letter the next day saying you're precious to the Lord and us.

God knew in 1984 when Dr. Davis came to visit me in the county jail that he'd be someone I'd need spiritually to stand with me. God knew in 1985 when I first met Bro. David Harmon that he'd help keep me encouraged and God knew in 1993 when Bro. Sonny handed Grandmother Miller that magazine to read that they would become family and spiritual strength for me over the years that I would be in prison.

God knew in October 1987 when I was fighting a spirit of suicide. I felt guilt and despair because of the pain I had caused so many people due to the terrible crime I had committed. I went through a period of months when I felt unworthy of Christ's grace and mercy and though I prayed for days on my knees, I couldn't seem to break through all my doubts that He loved me and had forgiven me.

As I read from 1 John 1:8-9, I told the Lord that I would stay on my knees and by faith in those scriptures, I would believe Him and not what I was feeling. I stayed there by my bed in prayer until the early hours. The despair and depression I had for months climaxed that night. Then a breakthrough came and in sweet tears of relief, He poured out His Spirit on me and strengthened me. The Holy Spirit broke that astounding temptation and I got up and wrote this song/poem:

He Carries Me Again
By Jimmy Windham

Many times in my life I stumble and I fall.
The heartaches seemed so heavy through it all,
But I know of a Shoulder I can lean on when I give in,
For He's my precious Savior and He carries me again.

Chorus:
He carries me again, yes, He's my dearest friend.
I can't take another step, Lord, Satan says I must give in
My cross seems so heavy; in my own strength I'll never win,
Then He carries me again.

On this road I'm now walking, many people are passing by.
They're always in a hurry, and it makes me wonder why

There's no time for Jesus, no kind word for a friend,
No time to smell the flowers; then He carries me again.

When my life was so broken, and it seemed I was alone,
Jesus wrapped His arms around me and gave me strength to carry on.
I can see down this road now; I have a friend 'til the end,
For He's my precious Savior, and He carries me again.

Many nights by my bedside as I go to God in prayer,
I seek my Lord for comfort and He always meets me there.
In words so kind and gentle, in a way I understand
He taught me just to trust Him and to hold His gentle hand.

Then in June 1989, this song came to me:

The Battle is the Lord's
By Jimmy Windham

Today's battle was so mighty I couldn't even lift my hands.
My strength seemed to vanish; around my head I felt the bands.
The enemy of my soul did his best to take control,
But tonight, down on my knees I felt the victory.

Chorus:
The battle is the Lord's, just trust Him and you'll see
He'll make a way for you; He's made a way for me.
The battle is the Lord's, the victory you'll see.
Your armor is God's Word, and the victory is on your knees.

When it seems Satan has you in a snare beyond control,
On your knees you'll find the Savior, He'll be there to guard your soul.
His joy is your strength; if you've sinned, then just repent
For in the mighty name of Jesus for your soul His blood was spent.

If you feel broken hearted and your strength is almost gone,
Turn your heart to God your Savior, then you'll know you're not alone.
His love is never-ending and his grace He'll freely share.
You'll find He'll never leave you, and His love is forever there.

If you're facing these kinds of trials and going through the fire of affliction and can't seem to find a way out, then I pray my words today in my songs will give you the answer and help you find peace in our loving Savior's words. Read 1 John 1:8-9 and stand on those scriptures. I did! And it brought me through my despair, pain and sorrows.

You say God did that for you? I say, "Yes!"

He'll show you He loves you if you'll bow down before Him and confess your sins and let Jesus come into your heart. God is Love and God loved you so much that He let His only Son die in your place so you can have eternal life, but the choice is yours. He won't *make* you come to Him. Why don't you do this right now? I am praying for you as is everyone else who has read this book!

Has it been hard to do 34 years? Surely so! There've been times that I've felt so alone and burdened that I prayed and asked God to take me home. A scripture says, "Weeping may endure for the night but joy comes in the morning." God's Word is true. The next day I was again able to go on.

If someone reading this book is in prison and is going through some of the things that I've experienced, I will tell you that you can make it. Just put your trust in God to answer your prayers. If you aren't a Christian, just get on your knees now and repent of your sins and ask Jesus to come into your heart. He won't refuse you. Now find a place to fellowship with other Christians. God bless you ALL! I hope and pray that anyone reading this book who *is* a Christian will pray for me that one day the victim's brother will forgive me for my terrible crime against his family and will one day let me go home to my family.

So, in closing this is what I've felt led to write. I pray this book has blessed you and I pray it has changed some people's minds and they've turned to Jesus. He's coming soon!

God bless you all, I remain, a prisoner of Jesus Christ.

Jimmy Windham SCDC #127054
Lee C.I. F6-2253
990 Wisacky Hwy.
Bishopville, SC 29010

Remember: Jesus Christ came to save sinners of Whom I *was* chief.